A Common Thread:

Stories of our oneness

*To Karen,
Thanks for your appreciation of my stories!
Blessings, fondly,
Elizabeth*

Elizabeth Kaites

iUniverse, Inc.
New York   Bloomington

A Common Thread: *Stories of our oneness*

iUniverse books may be ordered through booksellers or by contacting:

iUniverse
1663 Liberty Drive
Bloomington, IN 47403
www.iuniverse.com
1-800-Authors (1-800-288-4677)

Because of the dynamic nature of the Internet, any Web addresses or links contained in this book may have changed since publication and may no longer be valid.

ISBN: 978-1-4401-7127-7 (sc)
ISBN: 978-1-4401-7128-4 (ebk)

Printed in the United States of America

iUniverse rev. date: 9/22/2009

ACKNOWLEDGEMENTS

To my husband, family, and friends who have shared, encouraged, and enriched my journey.

Special thanks to my granddaughter, Eva O'Leary Chidester, whose drawings of people became the cover of my book. To Genna Herron, whose friendship, editing, and computer skills were invaluable. Yvonne and Hank Hellman's attention to my photos enriched this book.

Thanks to Kate Robinson of the Prescott Professional Writers who was my primary editor and the one who urged me to dig deeper into myself. Sharon Keene first encouraged me in her critique group to publish my stories. Wilma Gore, Jeri Castronova, Sydney and Jim Mitchell, Rev. Charli Tupper, and Vaughn Delp all read and critiqued. My dear friend Suzanne Walker invited me to attend her Wednesday writers group and I began to believe that I could give voice to my stories. Earl Merrifield was special with his computer know-how, as well as his caring.

With gratitude to my husband, John, who challenged me to publish my stories and supported my time away from our life to do the work. Mostly to Spirit, Who opened my eyes and heart to the Oneness of all and our Common Thread.

CONTENTS

Preface

Part Three – Voices of Inspiration

PREFACE

It wasn't until an astrologer told me that I was living the life that I seemed to be created for that I thought about my stories. She had also posed the question, "But, are you writing?"

I replied, "My mother was a gifted writer, but I just write human interest stories."

Her second question, "Why do you think you chose her to be your mother?" stopped me cold. Upon reflection, I realized that Mother wrote about incidents in daily life that touched her. My stories are about people who have inspired me and, oh yes, have touched me. So, I joined a small writing group, and it was no coincidence that they said my stories touched them and should be published.

"But, what is the common thread?" I asked and, "why would they interest anyone but me?"

Their reply, "We love your stories." That started me on this journey.

I believe the Common Thread starts from my understanding that we are all one. I think of the Divine as the ocean and each of us as a drop of water, and that we are all part of the same energy. I have realized that each of my stories is an example of how particular people, who I have encountered in my life, are like me in some way and, therefore, like you. Their stories could be our stories. They touched my heart because I felt one with them. I believe they will do the same for you. As you read each story, a special part of your heart will say, "Yes, I know," and, "That person is like me." And I hope that you will come to know and understand yourself better because of this connection.

For much of my life I have been involved with people, sometimes as a part of their growth and healing. If my purpose in life and, perhaps, yours is to make the world a better place, to be a healing influence to others whenever and with whatever we can offer, we will have succeeded. I have experienced that when "the other" and I are on the same wave length, we are energetically connected, and when, also, connected with the Divine, healing can occur. Knowledge about the truths of life is not enough ... we must each do our own work to raise our consciousness, and then live those truths. These stories give us a glimpse of people living their truths in everyday ways.

I hope you will see in these stories how each of us is a vital thread in another person's tapestry. Our lives are woven together for a reason.

Many times I have asked why I have such a passion for travel. But I do believe that meeting people from different cultures can reinforce our understanding of Oneness. Glimpsing into their lives can inspire you to see yourself in a new way that can be healing mentally, spiritually, and physically. Change can be as simple as being less judgmental, more compassionate, or seeing a blocked or broken place that has prevented you from moving forward in higher consciousness.

Open your heart to the folks in these stories. Laugh, cry, relate, and be inspired. Spend time thinking of similar stories in your own lives and, in so doing, realize the common thread in us all.

Part One:
Voices of Family

WATER AND ME

A re you more of a mountain person, a lover of the desert, or a water person? All my life I have been drawn to water; I feel connected to Spirit there. If we are created in Spirit's image and our bodies are mostly water, no wonder I come to the water for communion with the Divine.

My earliest memories of bodies of water larger than my bathtub, the local swimming pool, or the lazy river that trickled through our inland town, were of our summer visits to Mama and Papa who lived near the Chesapeake Bay. Mama's father was a boat captain on the Bay and she grew up on Tilghman Island. A must during the visit was our day with Patty Ann. She was my brain-damaged cousin who would get so excited about our visit that she rocked back and forth singing, "Betsy's coming and we're going on the big boat."

Joining the crowd waiting to board the excursion boat to Tolchester, picnic baskets in hand, was our favorite ritual. I loved that day as much as Patty Ann. I can still see the sparkling water, hear the organ music, smell the fish, and drool over the rosy, red watermelon we ate for our lunch. I connected at a deep level with Patty Ann on those days.

In later years, my husband and I often volunteered to take the youth fellowship at church to Ocean City, an affordable way to spend a few days at the beach with our young family. We all body surfed, swam, jumped waves and, generally, loved being in the water. I never tire of watching the waves curl and foam as they rush to the shore.

I fled to the water to heal after the break-up of my marriage. One night as I sat on the balcony of our rental unit, kids asleep and tears flowing, I prayed. As I opened my eyes, the moonlight had created a path, straight as an arrow across the water to my broken heart. I felt connected to Spirit and healed that night at the water's edge.

Soon after, a former Navy man came into my life. We went sailing on our honeymoon and to this day go to the ocean at least once a year to re-connect to water. I no longer feel alone and we grow in our closeness to Spirit.

Friends who owned a travel company asked my husband and me to lead a tour, *In the Footsteps of St. Paul*. One of the members of the group was a young minister. I noticed him putting drops from a small bottle of essential oils on his wrist before we went to Corinth. "What is that for?" I asked.

"Oh, this is a liquid flower essence that will heighten my awareness of a spiritual experience."

I was fascinated and asked if he would share. He and I looked for a spiritual experience at Philippi, Thessalonica, Delphi, Corinth, and other sites spoken of in the Bible. Nothing special happened until one day in Turkey. We stopped at a beach where young soldiers from New Zealand had been massacred as they left their ship for the beach below a high cliff. The Turks were up on the cliff. The young soldiers below were easy targets. None survived. Most of our group scurried up the hill to see the view or anything to get off that beach. I, however, had an overwhelming feeling of stranded souls still left on that beach. I prayed that they ascend to the Light. This wasn't the spiritual experience I had expected; but, then, is it ever?

One year I was interviewed for a newspaper article that featured my photograph. The writer's words included, "Her eyes have the look of the ocean and she peers into others' souls with an awareness of Universal Spirit."

Whenever I need to clear out old feelings and express who I was created to be, I head for the water. I believe our challenge is to remain open to Spirit, listen for guidance, and respond as best we can.

While it is true that I love living in the mountains and enjoy the quiet beauty of the green hills and trees, love the warmth and spaciousness of the desert, there is a special connection to Spirit between water and me.

THE NAME GAME

With great excitement, my carry-on stuffed with a bottle of good Italian red wine, homemade cranberry bread, and a MP3 player for my granddaughter, I left Phoenix, Arizona, bound for a visit to Drumshambo, Ireland. My older son, an art professor at Penn State University, was there with his Irish wife and their fourteen-year-old daughter, on a year's sabbatical. They had bought a tiny country cottage on one-and-a-half acres several years before and had spent summers fixing it up. My younger son and six-year-old daughter met me in Atlanta where we boarded our Delta flight to Dublin, ready for a great time with Paul and his Irish connections.

After an all-nighter, we deplaned in Dublin and eagerly approached the smiling Irish immigration officer. His red face, glistening white hair, green uniform, and impish eyes just looked the picture of the friendly welcome we were expecting.

"And where are you staying while in our fair land, Mrs. Kaites?"

"Oh, I'm going to Drumshambo, in County Leitrum, where my son, Paul Chidester, is living." The smile changed to one of concern as the computer screen did not show a Paul Chidester.

"Does he have another name?" the official asked.

"Just Paul David Chidester, married to Helen O'Leary," I replied.

"Well, he's not registered. Do you have his phone number?"

"He's probably upstairs waiting for us," I helpfully replied, sure this would be straightened out when the official spoke to Paul. There was no answer to the page.

"Since Paul had a three-hour early drive to get here by 8:00am, perhaps he's not arrived yet," I offered. "Paul had told his brother and me to get a cup of tea and wait if he wasn't here when we arrived." I was beginning to think this wasn't the reception we had looked forward to.

The official turned to my son, Steve, a bearded young man with a guitar strapped to his back who lived in the Colorado mountains. "And what's your name?" he asked this father who was trying to calm his restless six-year-old.

"Steve Storm," he replied.

I hastened to explain that Steve had changed his name when he and his wife gave birth to their first child in the middle of a Colorado storm. I was proud that he didn't think it fair that she had to give up her last name when they married, so they chose a new name for their new family.

By now the official looked askance, becoming convinced that he was on to something irregular, possibly a terrorist cell.

A phone call to Paul's cottage got Mary Murphy, who was visiting and caring for Paul's daughter while her mother was in India preparing for an art show. Mary Murphy didn't know anything about Paul and Helen's registering with the Irish police when they arrived in Ireland.

I was shocked and beside myself when the official turned to me saying, "Well, Mrs. Kaites, I'm sending you, Steve Storm, and child back to the States on the next flight in one-and-a-half hours."

Fortunately, Mary Murphy had thought to get the official's name, Dennis Caffries. Paul arrived at the Dublin Airport and received the page. With trembling voice, he told Dennis that he had never been told that he had to register with the Irish Police. No, he didn't have his passport with him, not imagining that he'd need it to pick up his mother and brother at the airport.

"Well, you're not registered, son, and I'm sending your mother and brother back on the very next plane to the States," asserted Dennis. By then, we were all frantic and puzzled as to what to do.

Back in the cottage, Eva, my granddaughter, had awakened and heard Mary's upsetting story. With a "what's the big deal" teen-age look, she said that because her mom was Irish, her dad didn't have to register with the Irish Police when they arrived.

A call to Dennis and a search from Eva into the pink wall cupboard back at the cottage, produced the necessary information. So, an hour later, Dennis flashed his Irish smile and welcomed us to Ireland, whoever we were, whatever our names were.

Three days later, Paul returned to the airport to pick up Helen, who was returning from India. He had told her on the phone of our experience, and my daughter-in-law was primed. She approached the only white-haired, red-faced official with her own grin. "I hear you almost deported me mother-in-law the other day."

"Would that have been a good thing?" Dennis asked. As Helen laughed he offered, "Well, for a few bob, we could have done it right!"

WRITING MY MOTHER'S STORY

For the longest time I avoided writing because my mother was a writer, and my career was in psychology. She never wrote a book, but this English major wrote memorable letters to her friends, and was forever putting clippings from articles that inspired her into a box. She looked forward to the day when she gave herself permission to actually WRITE, and stop ironing and taking care of my father in his retirement boredom. Sadly, that day never came.

One day a psychic told me that I was living the life I was meant to live except, she asked, was I writing? I relayed this to my husband who replied, "You are just like your mother — you talk about writing, but never do much with what you DO write."

Chagrined, I realized that while I had written a children's play that was produced, a newspaper column for two years in a community paper, none of that was WRITING.

Responding to the challenge, I started compiling some of my

"stories" and joined a writing group. When these writers informed me that my short stories were really "first-person essays," I began to realize that my mother's writing and mine were very much alike. So I am including one of her essays in my collection. And, when this book is printed, we both will be published, like real WRITERS.

WHAT'S WRONG WITH THIS PICTURE?
By Helen Powell

Remember when we used our skill at solving "what's wrong with this picture?" instead of crossword puzzles? Since last spring when I went home, heartsick, from a concert at our high school, the need for correcting what I felt was a great wrong kept gnawing at my conscience.

One evening in early April, 1961, a group of about sixty-eight of our town's young people presented a concert for the community. They had rehearsed for weeks. The day before the scheduled public performance, my son had come home bursting with happy enthusiasm.

"I think you will enjoy it, Mother, because the kids in school just clapped and clapped when we sang for them. They didn't want us to stop. We're going to have to be sure to have encores ready for the evening performance."

But the public, for some reason — a card party benefit for one — just didn't attend. The pitiful applause was too weak to even raise the curtain once. We went away, leaving a fine group of young people behind a closed curtain, stunned, disappointed, and unbelieving.

I could not rid my mind of a question, "If, when these young people give of their very best, and they meet with repeated failure to receive recognition and attention from those to whom they look for guidance and concern, might not some of them resort to other ways of gaining our attention?"

We hear of juvenile delinquency, emotional problems, and poor values in our youth. Might good attendance at events like this school concert do a lot to prevent these problems? The most important thing we can do is to give our children a feeling of support from family and friends. So, please, next time think before you go to a fun event for you, like the card party, and neglect your child's activity.

At the bottom of my son's concert program was their warm wish for the audience, "May you leave with a song in your heart."

9

It has occurred to me that this is the only time Mother sent her writing to anyone other than a friend. This article was included in her Goucher College's alumni magazine. So I got to thinking about us. Is our writing alike as I said at the beginning of this piece? And are we more alike in what we choose to write about than I realized while she was living?

My musing is about *being* and *doing*. I think about Mother. She was an English major, but I don't remember her reading much; perhaps a new poetry book that a college friend or my grandmother would send at Christmas. Mother spent her time dealing with the dirt in a small Pennsylvania coal town and the many family chores.

I, on the other hand, while growing up would retreat to my room, book in hand, and have to be called at least twice before coming down for dinner. I had read all the books in our small town library before reaching seventh grade, and remember begging to be allowed to check out adult books. I think back to how Mother would excuse me from doing the dishes when she knew I was deep into a story. She became busy *doing* and gave me the gift to work on *being*. With the perspective of time, I also credit many of my values to her. She cared about fairness, justice, values, and spirituality.

I think about Jesus, our example of how to live. He told Martha that while she was busy *doing*, it was just as important for sister, Mary, to sit at his feet and *be*. There were times when he retreated to meditate and pray, and others when he *did*, and healed.

Where am I going with this? Well, it seems to me that I want to be a model of being *and* doing. Perhaps this collection of observations of folks and events in my life will let my children and others know that I *did* something with my writing, as well as my life.

And, Mother, may you have a song in your heart because one of your writings is included in this published book.

DON'T SPEAK TO STRANGERS

I n the late 1800s, Great Uncle Ben took Mary Venable Cox, his niece, to the train bound from Virginia to New York. He had raised her since her parents' death and he took his protective role very seriously. "Now Vennie, don't speak to any strangers and, by all means, avoid eye contact with any men," he said sternly, making certain she looked him straight in the eye.

The train hadn't pulled out of the station before Vennie, my grandmother, was deep in conversation with a strange man seated in her compartment. She wanted to know all about the big city, home of Columbia University, where she was headed to study mathematics. Vennie was one of a group of bright Southern college graduates to whom Northern universities had offered graduate scholarships. This was part of the attempt to rebuild the South after the Civil War. Her elders expected her to return and teach in a Southern college and, like a good Southern girl, listen to the men in her life.

Vennie returned to teach math at the Virginia Normal School where she met my grandfather, John Chester Mattoon. He was an artist who had won a scholarship to do graduate study at the Sorbonne. But he'd declined the scholarship for his widowed mother, who begged him not to leave her. He went into teaching instead and taught industrial arts, first at the Normal School, and later moved his wife, Vennie, and my mother, seven-year-old Helen, to the University of Indiana. When the University cut the Industrial Arts Program from their curricula, the family moved back to Maryland and moved in with John's mother. Vennie survived the increasing intrusion into her marital life as her mother-in-law kept the family accounts. John designed wrought-iron gates for estates and did some painting on the side.

John's persistent cough was diagnosed as lung cancer and the family sold their city home and moved to a hilltop country house in Woodstock. Grandfather painted, while Vennie spent her days caring for both Great-Grandmother and Grandfather, tending her children, raising chickens, making and selling doll clothes, and refinishing antiques.

When the time came for college, Vennie's two children took the train at the bottom of the hill and rode into Baltimore City where they had college scholarships. Friends came from Baltimore City on Sundays for Vennie's fried chicken and biscuits. She was a "survivor" in that she took what life gave her and managed to live with purpose and joy.

Vennie's daughter, my mother, met a chemist, married on the front lawn at Woodstock. Mother said that the daily train came right at the end of the service and tooted its whistle for all to cheer. I was four and living with Mom and Dad in Baltimore City when Grandfather Mattoon died. When my brother and I were older, we would come to Woodstock in summers and explore the hillside for Indian caves and pretend we lived back in time.

When we returned from our journeys, Grandmother had treats and games set out on a walnut oval table that I now treasure having in my home. She told us the story of how the table was saved from destruction, hidden in the barn of Great Uncle Ben's plantation when the Northerners burned their way South. I was told that Stonewall Jackson had nicked the table with his sword when he sat with Great-Grandfather Mattoon and General Lee years before.

Grandmother's nearest neighbor and friend, Mabel Herbert, had come from New York City to retire on the Woodstock hill. She had nursed many a celebrity at the sanitarium for alcoholics where she worked. On summer visits, I loved to run to her house down the lane, sit on the porch swing, pet one of the tabby cats, and listen to her stories. Vennie sometimes helped Mabel and her other country neighbors with their income tax returns, scribbling figures while sitting at her table.

She interested my brother in stocks at an early age and was always the best help with my math courses. I loved it when Grandmother would start the day with baking breads. She let me knead the dough and put the cinnamon into the rolls. We did this on a cloth spread out on the multi-purpose table. Each evening after the dishes were cleared, washed, and put away, someone always brought the Chinese Checkers board out to the table. This historic table represented welcome, good food, games, conversation, and, most especially, love.

I don't know whether my love of storytelling came from Grandmother, Mabel, or both. I fancy that I take after my grandmother in many ways. Not in math ability, for heaven's sake, but in her adventurous spirit, love of cooking and travel, interest in teaching, and, most especially, her independence. When one of my professors took a group of college students to Europe and I pleaded with my parents to allow me to take my summer job earnings out of the bank, Grandmother said, "Don't listen to your dad's objections or your mother's belief that you will need the savings for a car after college, go. It will open up the world to you." She slipped a hundred-dollar bill, her total monthly pension, to me as I left. She and I had many conversations when I returned about the differences and similarities in the people, cultures, architecture, history, and arts of Europe.

I've survived the challenges that life has brought me as Grandmother did, with the optimism, faith, love of family, and the ability to land on my feet. After a divorce, I earned my way through graduate school and then worked to put all four children through fine colleges. I dated, and later married, a stranger I met on a blind date. At one point, I accepted chickens as payment for counseling a farmer's wife. I have nursed my mother, father, and brother as they became ill and died, all the while working and finding joy in life. Friends, children, and grandchildren have always enjoyed my home-cooked meals.

We play Chess and Monopoly rather than Chinese Checkers on Grandmother's table now. I have replaced the old oak chairs, whose cane seats became torn and broken, with other antique chairs that have leather seats. My husband loves the table and we enjoy sharing its history with guests, pointing out the probable sword nick that Stonewall Jackson made. There are photo albums of my travels resting in the closet, bread baking in the oven, and paintings of Woodstock gracing our antique-filled home.

As you can see, Grandmother Vennie has influenced my world in many different ways. There are times when I curtail my independent spirit to ease family relationships, as Grandmother did. But most of all, like her, I'm always ready for a train or plane ride and a good conversation with a stranger.

A VERSION OF REALITY TV

I t was our annual trek up the Colorado highway to our son, Steve's, house. He and his family live at the end of a thirteen-hour road trip from Prescott, Arizona, to Crestone, Colorado, an alternative lifestyle community. Some would say that it is the Sixties revisited; others say it is a place where artists and spiritual folk can afford to live. The more modern conveniences, such as microwaves, two-bathroom houses, and televisions, are not usually found.

We awakened our first morning to the sound of a whistling tea-kettle, the dog scratching on our door, the grandkids cycling through the one bathroom, and Steve firing up the pot-bellied stove. With gratitude and a helping hand from my husband, I got up from the futon to begin the day.

Our daughter-in-law, Anikke, was doing her yoga in the only open space in the family room before heading out to feed the horses. Steve had just finished serving French toast when the front door opened to admit a bearded man holding a pair of cross-country skis. It hadn't snowed overnight; he had come to ask Steve if he could leave the skis until he came back to town. He was looking for a town with jobs. Crestone was full of Ashrams, Buddhist temples, Stupas, charter schools, artists, and alternative healers.

Anikke and Steve took us outside to see their newly built straw bale- and cobb-constructed greenhouse. Growing their own veggies helped stretch the need to drive forty-nine miles to the nearest large grocery store or pay the high fees for food at the local natural food store. Anikke headed off to join her crew of gals finishing an adobe floor while Steve showed us some kitchen cabinets he was building for a remodeling job in town.

The work was interrupted by a phone call from the local fifth grade school teacher asking Steve to go outside and watch the half of the Middle School students she had just left across the street from his house. She had planned a field trip for all the kids to see a surveyor who was working there, and she needed to drive her van back to school and get the rest of the students.

I hadn't finished washing the dishes before two puppies crashed through the front door in front of a young woman who smiled and said she was on her way to Denver, would be back in a few days, and she knew the pups would be no trouble. Since their mother was Steve's dog, she was leaving her pups with family. Our dog, Katie, was delighted to have two more animals to romp with. Maybe they could catch the stray kittens hiding under the porch, or knock over the guinea pig cage in the yard.

When the phone rang I was pleased, yet surprised, to hear Steve say, "No, not this time," when asked if they could care for what would have been the ninth animal.

I decided the way to depict this different world was to play Dave Letterman's Top Ten noteworthy events of the day:

Number 10: I was sent to pick up my grandchildren from school and drop a neighbor's kid off at his home. He managed to keep me from getting stuck in his driveway, but when I arrived home, Steve was patiently explaining to the angry mother that the stranger who had just dropped off her son was not a perpetrator, but his mother.

Number 9: We ate the kid's lunch since they insisted on making themselves quesadillas.

Number 8: Steve, already tired, asked for "time alone." We, babysitting, were pleased to tell the next person at the door that Steve wasn't available. The next time I looked out the window, I saw him talking to Steve, who had emerged from the teepee to see what the man needed.

Number 7: I suggested to the caller, who wanted to bring her daughter over to play with our granddaughter, that this wasn't convenient and patted myself on the back.

Number 6: I answered the door to find a large truck out front, the driver asking if Steve could help him get a big piece of equipment over to the repair shop, as it was too heavy for him to lift by himself. He left his two small kids in the house to play. I wouldn't have seen them, accompanied by our grandchildren, take off down the road if the dogs hadn't followed them and barked. I helped the "scared so much that her legs were wobbly" four-year-old from the stream bank, admonishing my six-year-old granddaughter that she doesn't leave the yard, especially not to take our small guests to the edge of the stream!

Number 5: Sitting on the front porch swing, listening to Steve play his guitar, we hear a loud bang from the horse trailer parked out front. Our grandson had tipped the stool over and now was stuck in the upper part of the trailer. Was I glad that Steve was there to sort out that one.

Number 4: The man who had left his kids to play came by and told us that his wife, who was on Anikkes's crew, wasn't home yet and he had to go somewhere else. His dog jumped out of the truck and joined our animal shelter.

Number 3: Did I mention that the two pups were missing?

Number 2: The mother of the two kids called, told me where she lived, and suggested that I bring the kids and dog home immediately, as she needed to get them ready for an evening school program. I found the house and she advised me that Anikke would be late coming home as the adobe floor was not setting up properly.

Number 1: I stopped at the expensive market in town, bought something to add to vegetables, sighed with relief to be greeted by the missing pups, and just entered the house in time to pick up the phone and say, "Why not?" to the invitation to attend a potluck and jam session at an artist's house the next night.

After dinner, the grandkids — freshly bathed and shining with cleanliness — angelic as they took turns reading from the latest Harry Potter book, and with many kisses, told us how much they loved having us there. I smiled with contentment.

After all, the dogs were curled up at my feet, exhausted from their day, Steve and Anikke were cuddling on the porch swing, and my husband pointed out the moon in the clear starry sky outside.

Maybe when we get back to our saner house and routine, we will watch Letterman's Top Ten and have our own list of reasons to stay home. But who needed television last week. We had a front-row seat at *Steve's Reality TV.*

A TIME TO DISOBEY

M y six-foot-two-inch-tall supervisor at the Baltimore City Welfare Department glared down at me and asked, "Why haven't you given up the childish name, Betsy?"

I sputtered as I explained to this girlfriend of one of the Baltimore Oriole pitchers, that I had been called Betsy since birth and only was named Elizabeth so my mother and father could call me Betsy.

"Well," this first boss explained with her haughty manner, "it is a nickname given to children and you are now a grown-up needing to make your own decisions."

I had heard that this woman was really hard and not much respected around the agency, and I realized that I had a challenging beginning to my career. I went home that night and told my new husband about the conversation and he thought it typical of psychologists. Those in the engineering field would never come up with such stuff, he told me.

As a fifteen-year-old, I had gone into the jail in the small town of

Connellsville, Pennsylvania, with the pastor of our Presbyterian Church to set up a counseling service for incarcerated youth.

I can't imagine now what help I could have been. They were almost always male, so at this first job as a college graduate, I was given the task of counseling young men, ages sixteen to eighteen, in the soon-to-be-disbanded Foster Care System for juveniles. They were to be seen in the adult courts in the near future. My, how the judge in the juvenile court room shook his head in bemused amazement when I appeared with one of my charges, who looked and seemed years older. I'm sure they were more experienced in the ways of the world than I, a newly graduated, blonde, twenty-two-year-old.

Tom was one of those nearing his eighteenth birthday. He came into my office, tobacco pipe in hand, and calmly sat down to meet yet another counselor. He had been in the system since age twelve. For the past four years, he had lived with one family in Sparrows Point, worked at Bethlehem Steel, and was the proud owner of a horse. I was impressed that he had taken care of this animal for the past two years. Tom told me that when he turned eighteen, he was going to enlist in the Navy and was looking forward to getting an education. I was happy that the service provided such an opportunity for young men like Tom.

I hardly recognized him when he came in for the first appointment after his birthday. Instead of a smiling graduate from his court-ordered visits to me, he was deeply depressed.

"They turned me down," he said.

As my mouth dropped, I managed to ask, "Why?"

"They said it was because I had a record."

I was astounded since I knew that at age thirteen, he had run away from a bad foster home, and held up a gas station attendant for eighty-seven cents, and had nothing since on his record.

After Tom left the office, I called the recruiter. He explained that while they accepted others with more serious records, Tom didn't have anyone to advocate for him.

"Would I do?" I quickly asked over the phone.

"Probably," was his reply.

My supervisor reminded me that on Page 238 of the Baltimore City Manual it said that counselors could not, under any circumstances, leave their offices. So, the next day I scheduled an appointment with the recruiter during my half-hour lunch. After all, my supervisor had advised me to grow up and make my own decisions.

The Navy recruiters were amused to see a young woman come in to plead Tom's case.

"We've never had a juvenile counselor come in before."

They heard only one long sentence before they smiled and said, of course, they would take him; they only needed someone to speak for him. I hurried back to the office, eager to call Tom. Instead, I saw a note on my desk to come see my supervisor's boss.

"Golly, what is this about?" I thought. Mr. Warfield asked me to explain my appointment with the recruiter. I told him that I believed Tom's four-year clean history, his employment with Bethlehem Steel, and, most importantly, his responsibility in caring for his horse, showed that he deserved an opportunity to further his education and achieve his dream of being a Navy man. He only needed someone to speak for him. No one else had and I could easily advocate for him.

"But, what about the Manual?" Mr. Warfield asked.

"I consider that an important guide in the larger goal of helping people. But in this case, I went on my lunch time," I said.

Mr. Warfield smiled and told me to please report to him in the future. He had just fired my supervisor.

SEVEN GOING ON THIRTY-SEVEN

His name is Jacob. He is seven years old. This curly brown-haired, brown-eyed darling runs his family and ours. How, you might ask? Well, let's start with the game of Risk. I thought it would be a welcomed change from Monopoly, which he always wins, since I had taught him to buy properties instead of hoarding his money.

Back to Risk. My turn and he says, "Now Grandmom, your best move would be..." He also believes he knows the latest rules for chess and won't hear of the regular rules I learned as a kid.

We went on a week's vacation to Indian Lake in Pennsylvania recently. My husband and I had rented a house on that lake one summer when Jacob's dad was a young boy, and our son wanted his sons to experience that cool, water adventure.

Quite a change from our dry desert land in Arizona. The rental was a wonderful house, complete with a motor boat and inner tubes. The tall oak trees shaded the deck overlooking the water and the trees were just the right distance apart for a hammock and a good novel.

We were sitting out on the deck when Jacob bounded up the stairs. With his insistent voice we heard, "Where is your son?"

My husband replied, "You mean your dad?"

"No," said Jacob, "I mean your son! He promised to take me on a tube ride."

Later that day, Jacob happened to notice the missing molar in my husband's mouth. "Wow, Grandad," he said, "how much did you get for THAT tooth?"

He didn't take it happily when his grandad informed him that the tooth fairy only paid for baby teeth. Sadly, we told this inquisitive soul that grownups have to pay when they lose big teeth and grandad hadn't decided if it was worth the price. Jacob had been the only one to notice, or comment, that it was missing.

Jacob wanted to try out the paddle boat that was upside down near the shore. He bounded up to the deck, "Grandad, we HAVE to turn over this boat."

After the initial attempt and discovery that the wooden paddle boat was quite heavy, my husband suggested that they wait for help.

"Grandad, we have to turn this boat over NOW."

"Dad," Jacob implored his father, who was busy tying up the motor boat nearby, "we have to turn this paddle boat over NOW." Dad sighed and came over immediately. He had been trained well.

Jacob's kindergarten teacher suggested during a parent/teacher conference that Jacob could become President ... if not of the country, then of something. She said he artfully directs the other kids in the class and she has to be aware of whether she is doing the lesson plan she wrote or has modified it according to Jacob.

Our neighbor says she always knows when Jacob is at our house — his voice has a commanding insistence to it. She, like we, though, seems to laugh about it. He is a likable kid, and surprisingly thoughtful. He notices when I am tired and suggests that I sit down for awhile. He finds ways to be helpful and is always looking for opportunities to earn money.

I'm wondering if Jacob is going on eight or, with his self-possessiveness, maybe thirty-seven. At the very least, Jacob is just himself ... a special seven-year-old grandson who I trust will grow up to be a fine thirty-seven-year-old.

TALKING TO THE BODY

T he phone rang and the message was chilling. My son, his nine-month pregnant wife, and our two-year-old grandson were hit head on by a drunk driver in Colorado, taken out of the destroyed car and air-lifted to a hospital in Grand Junction. Steve was in critical condition. With tears still flowing, I called the airlines to get on the first plane from Phoenix to Grand Junction. After packing a few things, I called our church to ask for prayers.

My daughter-in-law's father, who had arrived in Colorado from Vermont the night before, met my plane in the morning. He said, "We have a new granddaughter, born last night, and she and her mother are all right. Steve is serious but stable. His face is swollen, and he has tubes coming out of him, but you can still see that he is Steve." We hugged in mutual support and sorrow.

Tears slowly moved down my cheeks as I looked at my dear son, who appeared more like a Sumo wrestler than the man I knew and loved.

He tried to tear up when he saw me, but nothing worked on that part of him that was his face. The doctor came in and told us that he had scheduled surgery for the next morning, as Steve's head had lost enough blood for him to operate. Every bone in his face was broken; a tube fed him liquids since his jaw was broken and wired shut.

"There's still a lot of blood in his facial area," the doctor explained, "and what I am able to do in this first operation depends upon how much blood is in my way." The nurse reassured us that this thirty-two-year-old doctor had specialized in face reconstruction and had operated on many injured skiers.

I imagined hearing words from my healing energy teacher, Rosalyn L. Bruyere, flooding my head that morning. "Talk to the blood and visualize it down into his lower body."

I stood at the foot of Steve's bed and held his feet. He knew of my studies and he tried to shake his head to say thanks as my mind, energetically and with focused intention, pulled the blood from his head area towards his feet.

Surgery began at 8:00am. I kissed Steve and steadied myself as he was wheeled away toward surgery. I sought the chapel and started a combination of prayer and more talking to Steve's blood. I sent loving messages to his blood, and thanked it for the wonderful job it had done in keeping Steve alive, as well as circulating nourishment. However, now I was asking most of it to leave his head so the surgeon could do his work. The clock ticked away. I went to the nurses' station to ask if there was any word as to how the surgery was progressing.

"No one has come out," they replied.

First lunch-time passed, and then dinner-time came and went. I continued to talk to the blood, and thank it for its good work. At 9:00pm, the young surgeon came to find me. I saw the tired smile on his face.

"I was able to repair the entire face," he exclaimed. "I was amazed at how little blood was there." We both had grateful hearts as we went on our separate exhausted ways. Steve's healing progressed slowly, but well.

The doctor and Steve bonded even more when the doctor shared that his wife was pregnant. He admired Steve's beautiful newborn daughter as he had a two-year-old son and hoped for a girl this time.

My daughter-in-law's broken ribs hurt, but were healing. When I learned that she kept seeing the car heading right toward them on this narrow country road, some EMDR helped her release this sight and sleep through the nights.

The family had been returning from a baby shower that fateful Sunday afternoon when a trust-funder was driving home after an afternoon of drinking at his favorite bar. Friends who were in a car following Steve's took my two-year-old grandson, safe in the rear of the car because of his car seat, home with them. While Trevor proudly wheeled the cart with his new baby sister around the hospital corridors, and spent time with his mom, he didn't want to see his dad. His memory was of blood where his dad's face had been, as well as seeing his injured mom and dad being whisked away, high in the sky, to who knows where, in a helicopter. I took Trevor to the hospital gift shop and bought a toy helicopter, and we played how happy we were that one had come to take mom and dad to the hospital where they could receive help. Soon, Trevor, tentatively, walked into his dad's room and blew him a kiss.

Steve never had to have additional surgery, and I suggested to the young surgeon that he read about the benefits of "talking to the body energetically." He seemed interested.

When the doctor's baby girl was born, Steve drove to Grand Junction and delivered a coffee table that he had built, which was filled with gratitude for the loving care he had received.

Years later, my younger daughter had fibroid tumors in her uterus. She was almost forty years old and still held the dream of having a child. Her doctor was concerned about one of the fibroids, which was located in an awkward rear position. She told us that she hoped to be able to preserve Laurie's baby-making equipment, but this one fibroid worried her. Now, up in Boston at the hospital, I started to talk to the fibroid.

When the surgeon came out to see Joe and me, she was smiling. "Why, when I made the incision, that pesky fibroid was right there under my knife. Laurie should have no problem carrying a child!"

I said a prayer of thanks.

The next day in Laurie's room, as the doctor expressed her pleasure with the surgery, I started to tell her about talking to the fibroid. Laurie, knowing her doctor, glanced at me and said, "No, Mom." I shut up, as asked.

Dr. Bruce Lipton has done research confirming that each cell is a microcosm of the body, with its own brain and other organs. He has changed how he teaches young medical students about the biology of the body. But not every surgeon wants to hear about the help they can get by talking to the body!

A COURTIN' OMELET

Single mothers of four put out the cereal boxes and, on a good day, include some fruit and hope the little darlings can get the milk out of the fridge by themselves. As for me, I was out the door to work. My oldest was seventeen, so I felt comfortable that she could handle any minor crisis like, "there're no clean spoons!"

Life was pretty much about work, and then dealing with the needs and schedules of four school-aged kids. My ex was an elementary teacher in a private school for learning disabled children, so his Saturdays and Sundays were filled with projects. He was not much help to me.

A mutual friend introduced me to a male friend that she had met at a church seminar in another state. Our first date went well and I was invited up for the weekend. After a lot of arranging, I drove out of my driveway feeling both excited and leery. Did he really realize that this woman he enjoyed so much at dinner was the mother of four children, three of them teens? I worked as a guidance counselor at a high school, and there was college ahead for the children. But wait, don't get ahead of yourself. This is only a weekend to meet his friends and get to know each other better.

We talked a lot about values, priorities, and dreams. Spirituality was foremost for us both. We attended the same church denomination and were in leadership positions. He owned his own company and had been looking for a person with similar spiritual values to share his life. His friends seemed to like me and I liked them. We discovered similar interests. He had been single for seven years, so was quite capable in the kitchen.

I woke up Sunday morning to marvelous aromas floating up from the kitchen. Hurriedly I finished in the bathroom and descended the stairs to find the most beautiful breakfast awaiting me! No cereal, no "get your own dishes," but a smiling gentleman who pulled my chair out for me and gave me a morning kiss. My tea was steaming hot, the fruit carefully prepared, and then the omelet. Never had I seen such a lovely presentation! And there was the glass of red wine. For breakfast! I often say that this breakfast was the beginning of changing my life, as I married its creator and have enjoyed a partner in marriage, and in the kitchen, for the past thirty-two years.

MUSHROOM AND WINE OMELET FOR TWO

Sauté and set aside:

8 ounces of fresh mushrooms	¼ cup red wine
¼ cup butter	¼ teaspoon oregano
1 tablespoon Worcestershire sauce	¼ teaspoon garlic powder
Salt and pepper to taste	

Whisk four or five eggs. Pour into warmed omelet pan or skillet. When beginning to set, spoon half of the mushroom mixture onto one side of the eggs. With a spatula, carefully flip the plain side over top of the filling side. Remove to a plate and spoon one teaspoon of the mushrooms on top of the omelet. Toast or a muffin completes this picture.

Happy courting!!

I'M TOO BUSY TO LOVE YOU

I sat at the computer, putting the finishing touches to a story. Katie, my dog, jumped up and pawed my arm. Unable to type, I rubbed her back and face and heard myself say, "I'm too busy to play with you now." Startled, I was transported back to my childhood when, too many times, I'd heard those same words from a parent. Only, I heard, "I'm too busy to listen to you now," or, "I'm too busy to spend time with you now."

Seeking treatment for a back that spoke to me, painfully, through the years, I heard the chiropractor ask what event I could recall that happened in my life just before my back started to hurt. I flashed back to a time when I was twelve and in charge of my younger brother.

We were relegated to the tiny back porch while my parents painted the floor of the front porch. The front was our window on the world. Cars and people passed on the sidewalk and street; there was lots of grass to play on. It was not boring and bleak like the back porch.

Since my mother always put a harness on my brother to control his movements, I thought it would be fine to take him out to the grassy front lawn where we could see the world pass by.

I was not prepared for my parents' anger. That day I decided that I would always do what they said, even if I disagreed. It would certainly prevent such outbursts and my sad feeling. And so that's how I lived my life with most everyone, for many years.

When my chiropractor asked what I needed that I didn't receive back when I was twelve years old, I heard myself say, "Love and respect for my opinion."

"Well," he said, "every time your back starts to hurt, give it love and respect." So, after years of braces, pain pills and visits for chiropractic adjustments, I now give my back love and respect. It hardly hurts at all, and when it does, I quickly give it love and respect and the pain lessens or stops.

You guessed it. I stopped my typing and gave my dog love and attention!!

A GRAND SPECTACLE

Today I was looking in a book of poems that belonged to my Grandfather Mattoon. He wrote many, so I guess I come from a long line of writers. I'd like to share one of his poems written in July, 1901, about the Pan-American Exposition.

Toward the close of the day
I wended my way
To the court where assembled the throng
When the daylight's last beam
As a voice in a dream,
Fades away like the echo of song.

As I gazed on the sight
Of the day's waning light
The strains of sweet music I heard.
Then, faintly, a glow

As of light, burning low
Crept o'er all like a soft whispered word.

A hush quickly fell
Like some mystic spell
O'er the throng, while the music came stealing
But gathering in might
To usher the light
Into radiance great beauty revealing.

Mid the glory of light
From the left to the right
I gazed with a feeling of awe
And, with half closed eyes
I could near realize
That 'twas Paradise there I saw.

And the music, so grand
By the masterly band
Seemed to us as a heavenly chorus
Of angelic voices
When Heaven rejoices
With those who have gone on before us.

Nor should I neglect
To note the effect
Of the beautiful fountains there playing
In that ocean of light
Almost dazzling the sight
Like gems, their great beauty displaying.

I can hardly express
The mighty impress
Of this wonderful scene on my being
But my thoughts wander far
Beyond the last star
To the source — the Father — all seeing.

J. Chester Mattoon

So, in this collection of stories of our oneness, I add another.
Grandfather speaks of light, travel, spirituality ... all grand spectacles.

LIFE'S PATHWAY

He smiled up at me when I opened the front door of my house. His dad and I were to be married and he had arrived from out West for the ceremony, and to meet me and my children. After my boys had taken him out to meet our goats, a visit to the boys' rooms, and a good meal later he announced, "Dad, these are my kind of people."

This twelve-year-old was still living with his mom and step-dad when, on my first visit, I learned about the candy- and gum-selling racket he had organized in school. This charming entrepreneur had developed a way to supplement his allowance. He continues with this quality today, only now it involves multiple companies, higher values, and more substantial rewards.

Shortly after our marriage, he chose to live with us. I discovered that, like his dad, he was not a good reader and spelling was not his strength. However, he had developed a keen memory and with his ever-present charm, it was easy to find girls to type his papers.

With his organizational abilities, he planned Senior Cut Day. The High School Principal bet me that he would be the keynote speaker at his twenty-fifth reunion.

But, I'm getting ahead of myself. One day after school, I heard this tenth grader pacing the upstairs floor, and reading the sports section of the paper as a radio announcer would. Recognizing this positive interest of his, I managed to get him on as a gopher at the local radio station. His dad advised him to learn every job there, and soon he volunteered to take the graveyard shift when the regular announcer was on vacation. He filled in for others, and eventually helped put himself through law school by being the TV weatherman.

His step-sister challenged me when she and he would come home for a break from college. She would be in the laundry room doing her clothes, I would be doing his. He always had a conflicting, more important, appointment. His wife tells me there's been no change.

I used to gulp when I saw him put a twenty-dollar bill in the Sunday offering. "You taught me to tithe and be generous," would be his retort. Today he supports many causes and tithes his time by coaching his son's sport's teams.

One day he drove by the church where he and his wife were married. Noticing its stained, chipped exterior, and hearing about the lack of funds, he mailed a check the next day. Money and opportunities to do good find him, and he listens.

As a state legislator, he asked each lobbyist to detail why he should support a bill, in five minutes or less. His early reading difficulties enabled him to learn with his ears, his radio work encouraged him to be succinct, and his spiritual home to measure success in terms of service to others.

His dad and I are delighted that family is most important to him. While others see him as lucky, he has always visualized and expected life to be positive. No goal has been as important as being in God's plan for his life. He walks away from seeming disappointments, looking for what lies ahead, sure that it will be good.

Where am I going with this piece? It's just an example of how a boy's optimism in meeting the challenges of his parents' divorce and his dyslexia, together with a desire to do God's will, developed into a spirit of service. That, along with charisma, can get you down life's pathway as good as any way.

LIKE-MINDED FOLK

I t was twenty years since they had spent a summer together. In those days they were like-minded guys, taking great care to build a boat with hand tools and talking about their love of wood, the earth, and their life values. Steve was a student at the College of the Atlantic in Maine, who had a summer job working for Bill, a "down Easterner." They were building a pinky schooner named the *Summertime* near the coast with plans from the Smithsonian. The pink-sterned hull with schooner rig was used in the New England fishing fleet prior to the Revolution. These two guys hadn't seen each other since Steve left Maine for life in Colorado.

Now Steve had brought his family, vacationing with the in-laws in Vermont, to have a day sail on the schooner. He and Bill talked about life since that first summer years before. Steve learned how to build a galley then, and now he was building kitchens in Crestone, Colorado. Most were from refinished old barn siding. Bill had taught Steve how to respect old wood. They both rubbed old woods with love, and appreciated the earth which had created them. Both loved other natural materials, as well. Steve talked about his respect for straw bale and cobb construction, and the appreciation of residents in Crestone for alternative building.

Then as old salts do, the conversation turned to story telling. Bill laughed as he told Steve about the first race for the *Summertime*. It was one of one-hundred-fifty-four other vessels that raced from the coast of Maine to an island in the Atlantic. The *Summertime* hadn't been built to race; it was a work boat, kind of like Bill and Steve. It came in dead last. But Bill added, with a twinkle in his eye, "I think we snagged a lobster pot on the propeller and, perhaps, that had a little bit to do with our finish."

Steve told Bill about his lifestyle in Crestone, a small community at the foot of the mountains near the Great Sand Dunes National Park, known for its alternative building practices and spiritual retreats. There is one road in and out. His kids go to a charter school which ranked third in the state for academics last year. Amazingly, there were only four graduates and they all received scholarships. The family television is only used for videos, leaving plenty of time for riding lessons, hikes into the mountains, building projects, and outdoor adventures.

He shuddered as he related to Bill a car accident years before when their car was hit by a drunken trust funder and he was nearly killed. The settlement enabled him to buy a little ninety-year-old house for the family in Crestone. Bill shared that he used his trust fund money to finish the schooner.

Steve reminisced about his last night in Maine, that end of summer years before. He had wrestled with the decision as to whether to accept a job in a lighthouse there in Maine, which came with its own boat, or to go to Telluride, Colorado, get a job, live in a tree house, and play music.

Steve took the dinghy out to Soames Sound, a half-mile-wide inlet. It was a dark night with only a new moon overhead. This was a life-changing decision and he needed time alone.

His companion was a Native American flute his mother had sent him from Arizona. He stopped rowing and drifted with the tide as he played haunting melodies. Suddenly he sensed that he wasn't alone. There was something bobbing in the water off the side of his dinghy two feet away. He squinted, looking in the direction of the bobbing object. Trying to convince himself that there couldn't possibly be anything in the water way out where the tide had taken him, he continued to play for at least twenty more minutes. Suddenly a seal's head popped up close enough to see and the moonlight glistened off his smooth head. Man, animal, and the music seemed one.

It was a magical moment, and as a tear glided down his cheek, Steve's heart turned back to shore and to Telluride, with its musical opportunities. He was currently playing guitar in Colorado and teaching his musically gifted children. Crestone offers a lifestyle of spirituality, creativity, a community of service-oriented people, and the summer music festivals of Telluride are a four-hour drive away.

Bill shared that his life continued to be great there in Maine with his beloved schooner. Twenty years later, living far away across the United States, those two men, on a summer's day wearing their straw hats, discovered that they are still like-minded folk.

GETTING HOME WAS NOT MUCH FUN

I t took us four and a half hours to drive to Lake Powell and thirteen hours to return. Our family had enjoyed such a grand week-long house-boating adventure that we didn't even mind that the borrowed company van's air-conditioning wasn't operable. Memories of white sandy beaches, warm clear water, evening campfires under a blanket of stars, hikes to the Moki steps and petro glyphs, water-skiing on glassy surfaces between canyon walls, and tanned bodies who had shared lots of conversations, were still casting a rosy glow.

Our daughter's family had left Bullfrog Marina for the longer ride to Denver while we six started out for the shorter ride to Phoenix. As we descended from the cool pines of Flagstaff into the warmer Verde Valley, we heard an ominous sound, pulled to a stop, and stared at our flat right rear tire. Our first challenge was to find the jack (it was under the hood). The space in the large Suburban we had been so delighted to borrow was filled with luggage, coolers, tents, an inflatable boat with oars, fishing gear, food, sheets, towels, jugs of water, books, cameras, recorder with tapes, Pictionary, etc.; so was now a lot of work to unload and then reload, like a jigsaw puzzle, back into the vehicle.

My husband and brother removed the spare tire from under the mound of stuff and placed it on the wheel in just ninety minutes. We sighed with relief as we piled our sweaty bodies back into the van. Eager for the cooling breezes inside a moving vehicle, the silence was intense after the key in the ignition produced no welcome sound of a roaring engine. Back outside and only eight Good Samaritans later, we had a jump start for our dead battery, and once again, we were on our way.

We needed cool drinks, the spare needed air, and mother a bath-room, all provided by the gas station fifteen miles down the highway. Eager to get home, unpack, and cool off by our pool, we pressed on. A few miles from New River (forty miles from home), a horrendous noise caused us to drive off the road into the dirt-filled median and quickly get out of the smoking car. Closer inspection revealed a burst and ripped left rear tire — the exhaust pipe somehow had dug into the tire — and we viewed some damage to the exhaust system.

If you happened to have driven down I-17 that day and wondered what those two wilted older people were doing sitting in deck chairs amid the ants in the middle of the median on a hot summer's day, they were my parents waiting for the AAA wrecker to arrive from Black Canyon City. A motorist stopped, let us borrow his phone to call an employee to come and get the rest of us, and wished us well.

The tow truck came first, so Mother and I rode in the cab to give directions to my house, while my father and daughter rode in the tilted Suburban, and my husband and brother waited in the dusk, armed with a flashlight, to signal the employee who usually drives the Suburban, to bring them home.

"Sure is a heavy car to tow. I have to go real slow 'cause it's on my axle," droned the driver. We finally arrived home, just before 11:00pm, and I hurried into the house to listen to the message on the answering machine that would say my husband and brother had been picked up and were on their way to us. Again, silence. I called the employee's house, and found him at home, so sorry not to have found the two stranded men.

There was nothing to do but get a drink of water and head back to New River. Confident of recognizing the half-mile or so stretch of highway where we had left them, Dad and I circled twice before heading off the nearest exit, concerned about where in the world they could be. The sign pointed left into the town or right to gas. Choosing the right turn, we were led to gas pumps outside a roadside bar complete with blaring music inside, and bearded men with black leather jackets and motorcycles outside. I was grateful that Dad had insisted on accompanying me. Cautiously driving a bit beyond the open door and an outside phone, we heard a voice yell, "Come on in!"

As I looked in my rear view mirror, there was my husband, waving us in, jaunty in his Greek sailor's cap more appropriate for our morning at the lake, which seemed so very long ago. As we entered, the barmaid, whose boobs were quite visible above her denim overalls, shouted in delight, "I knew she'd find you. Sit down and join us for a beer."

Somehow, at midnight, hungry, not yet home, exhausted by the day yet relieved to be all right, it seemed like the thing to do.

Bottoms up!

I JUST BURIED MY BROTHER
NEXT TO MY PARENTS

David was six years younger than I; more like a child of mine growing up and then an adult best friend. Now his ashes, in a walnut box, were being placed next to our parents' remains in the family cemetery plot in Granite, Maryland. David's only son, Jeff, wiped a tear as he struggled to let go of the box and place it in the open grave. The parting was wrenching. Jeff was only twenty-two years old and still in need of his loving dad. They could talk about anything, and did.

I had picked up Jeff at the Washington airport when he returned home after flying for two days from Africa – his interrupted college graduation trip. David had wanted him to go as planned and didn't let him know how uncertain his remaining time would be. Jeff had seen that his dad wasn't well and debated going, but David's insistence won out. Jeff didn't know how much he would question that decision in the years after David's death.

I sat with David for ten days at the Hospice where he spent his last days and nights. Oh, how he fought to live. His eyes pleaded after his mouth could no longer produce words. I hugged and kissed him, as always. After Jeff arrived, he slept on the floor of his dad's room for the five days he had with him. That fifth evening, the nurse persuaded Jeff and David's partner to go out and get a proper dinner, while I agreed to stay with David. *Faure's Requiem*, a favorite of my brother's, was playing on the recorder, competing with the death rattle that was getting weaker and weaker. Then I heard them. Two black birds were on the window sill outside the room, cawing.

"David," I whispered, "Mother and Dad are outside waiting for you. It's all right to let go." And he did. I sat there while the nurse gently closed his big, brown eyes. I asked her to phone the restaurant and tell Jeff to come. As she closed the door, she advised me to sit quietly and treasure this sacred time with my brother. It was peaceful and quiet, a special time for prayer.

The cemetery was in Baltimore County at the Granite Presbyterian Church. It hadn't changed since the years when David and I would attend Sunday school there while visiting Grandmother Mattoon. It hadn't changed since David and I were there to bury our parents. Those of us there that day for David's burial sat in plastic white chairs behind the large gravestone with our last name engraved on one side and our grandparents' last name on the other. They were buried next to each other and there was a space for their only son, my uncle, and his wife. Both my mother and her brother had each lost a baby and those little markers completed the plot. I realized that with David's passing, I was the oldest living member of the family. I was grateful for my life NOW, for Jeff's, and those of my children's and grandchildren's.

As the cellist played her haunting piece and as the breeze played with our hair, Jeff turned to look at me with startled eyes. A raven was cawing, calling to us above the earthly music. It seemed to say, "Ha, ha, there is an afterlife after all!" You see, my brother never trusted in the part of religion that talked about a transition. Mom and I believed, but Dad and David had to be shown. Well, now he knows.

I miss my brother. We were the only ones to share our history. Who else could I talk to about the changes to the old Anchor Hocking Glass Corporation in Connellsville, Pennsylvania, where our dad was the chief chemist and we both worked during summer vacations from school. Why, they even turned our high school into a Social Security center. How about the elaborate lions now gracing the edge of our former home's driveway! Who did the new owners think they were, anyway?

I am grateful for the relationship I had with David, and the many memories. And, yes, I am grateful that he is no longer suffering. I do realize that his illness was many years ago and doctors have come a long way in managing Aids and prolonging life. However, I believe in Divine Order and David fulfilled his mission on earth. I also believe in the Oneness of all and know that David is sharing in the joys of Jeff's marriage, his nieces' and nephews' accomplishments, and my new venture of writing stories.

During an out-of-body exercise at a recent workshop, I was able to rise above my body and fly around on the ceiling. For a brief moment, I was sure that David grabbed my hand and flew with me. Part of me still feels connected to him. I believe that we are all connected. While it's a sad experience to have to bury your only brother next to your parents, I know that those were just ashes and that his spirit is alive and with me still.

A QUESTION OF JUSTICE

I sat in the front row viewing the parade of black caps and gowns walking slowly across the stage at the University of California's Berkeley campus graduation. My uncle was the second one called to receive his PhD diploma. Uncle Ray was eighty years old.

Originally, Ray's investigations into "The Just War" produced a monumental volume of nine-hundred-thousand words. By chiseling away many details, he reduced his dissertation to three-hundred-thousand words. One member of his Doctoral Review Team refused to accept his long and tedious academic opus and that one reader kept him from receiving his doctorate. It did not seem fair, much less just.

Ray Mattoon grew up in the country, across the hill from a Jesuit Seminary in Woodstock, Maryland, before World War II. He graduated from college and was ready to enter the seminary when the war started and he was drafted. After serving as a bombardier on many missions, he returned home, the sole survivor of his crew. His pre-war plan to enter seminary was dashed when, on his furlough, he rode a tractor with Woodstock farmer, Mr. Crum, and in their religious discussions, Ray decided that seminary would not teach him any more about God and spirituality than Mr. Crum had learned by observing and living his life close to nature. War had also challenged many of his earlier beliefs.

After he married my Aunt Thera, a lovely auburn-haired language teacher, he chose to stay in the military, went on to law school, and became an advocate general.

Once he retired from the military at age fifty-two, he pursued a doctorate in Philosophy at Berkeley. He was gifted with a brilliant mind, evidenced by his prestigious "Mensa" membership, an honor awarded to those who never failed to receive an "A" in every class they took. His mind was always in search of another scholarly one. When I married, still on my honeymoon, he called at midnight in an attempt to engage my new Greek husband in a discussion of the minor Greek philosophers. Ray was always disappointed when others didn't know as much as he did about a subject. John only knew of Plato, Socrates, and Aristotle and, then, by name only!

In his later years Ray joined the Outlook Club, a dinner group where members researched and gave speeches on weighty topics. Ray sent his papers to my mother and she pleaded with me to read them and offer some pithy comments so she would not disappoint this much loved brother of hers. My son, Paul, is a college professor in an art department. Since Ray's father was an artist and Ray also did some painting in his retirement, he and Paul had much in common and wrote long diatribes about this and that. Ray had finally found a member of the family capable of these mental exchanges.

Just before his eightieth birthday, Ray received a call from Berkeley informing him that he was to receive his PhD at the May graduation. The lone hold-out on his committee had passed on, and the new reader demanded that Ray receive his rightful degree. I flew from Phoenix to Oakland for the ceremony. My cousins planned a hotel luncheon celebration for the family afterward. Ray wondered why all the fuss; after all, what could he do with this degree now?

We each have the opportunity to see events as a closed door and then look for the open window to choices. Ray's discussion group benefited by his shared writings, he wrote wonderful histories of the Mattoon family, and he was an encourager for my children, as well as his own.

Ray died of Alzheimer's a few years later, but during his eightieth year he was fully aware and appreciative of his "Just Degree."

A Double Death

M y dad died twice. The first death was long and slow, a little at a time, tortuous to watch. The second was a gentle slipping away. Alzheimer's is like that.

Dad was working as the chief chemist for the Anchor Hocking Glass Corporation when he retired. His dad, also a chemist and a graduate of John's Hopkins University, lived to be ninety-six years old, sharp as a tack, until the end. My grandmother lived to be ninety-four and was clear as a bell, mentally. Mom died at age eighty-six, after a car accident when Dad got confused and ran a stop sign. Both cars were totaled, and Mom never recovered from the accident and the cancer discovered in that hospital. My husband and I agreed that Dad was too old to drive and we wouldn't agree to his pleas to own another car.

Like many families, we considered the numerous warning signs of beginning Alzheimer's as typical of old age. We had heard of others' parents who left the gas on after cooking, became forgetful about things, and lost interest in hobbies. We moved him into our home when he couldn't cope alone after Mom died. My husband became irritated when Dad listened in on phone conversations. I resented that he wouldn't retire to his room at the agreed upon time of 9:00pm; rather, always waiting until we went to our room, and that he depended upon us for everything. It became intolerable to have no privacy or life of our own.

We took Dad to visit an assisted-living retirement home, pointing out the many activities, the people his age, and the bridge groups. Dad was a master's level bridge player. He agreed to try living in the home, and we breathed a sigh of relief. The relief was short-lived, as each day brought a phone call telling us of a new problem. The bridge players said he couldn't remember the cards, he would wake up in the night and walk down the hall looking for breakfast, and he would often walk into someone's room, mistaking that room for his own.

Each day brought a new complaint from him: "They expect me to work in the rose garden," (I had told them he loved growing roses and had a green thumb) or, "You had better see what is going on in this place. I didn't get a meal today and they're running out of food."

Some days he thought I was part of the administration that ran the home. He started packing to return to our house. Each visit was heart-wrenching as I had to pacify or redirect him before I left.

The day came when I received a call from the director of the retirement home, giving me twenty-four hours to take him somewhere else. He had gone into the room next to his, and when the woman resident asked him to leave, he argued with her that it was his room and pushed her down. Her family insisted that my dad, this one-hundred-twenty-pound menace, be removed. I hired a nurse to be with him constantly while I searched for a residence that understood dementia. I made my daughterly feelings listen to the doctor's advice to "under no circumstances" take him back into my home. Such a tug of war raged inside me.

We had known that we had to find a community that specialized in dementia and Alzheimer's. A few weeks before we had taken him to our doctor, who asked him questions like: "Who is our president?

What did you have for dinner? How many fingers am I holding up?"
While he could still tell us stories about his past, and sometimes come
out with a good chemistry question for the nurses, he couldn't answer
the doctor's questions. It was his short-term memory that failed first.

We were thankful that the new residential home in town served
people with dementia and Alzheimer's and agreed to take him. He
first roomed with a retired minister; they were both intelligent, mild-
mannered men. I hadn't been gone fifteen minutes that first day when
the director had to move this normally sweet man into a private room.
She said that his swear words were heard up and down the hall,
shocking the minister. Dad hadn't sworn like that out loud, before or
later. I suspect he believed this move would be to my home, not this
new community, and he let the minister know his feelings about it.

Gradually, he lost interest in everything. Dad even forgot that he
liked a glass of wine with dinner. The nurse regretfully told me not to
bring any more in for him. He still perked up and grinned when I
brought our dog in. She licked his face, and it always brought a smile.
The nurses started calling him "Dr. Love" because he sparkled
whenever someone was affectionate with him. I hated the fact that
I pulled back from him when he referred to me as his wife, and tried
to lay his head on my breast. The staff suggested that I attend a
support group for caregivers.

Alzheimer's is so difficult because it lasts as long as the body
does, and Dad had good genes. We worried that the estate he
thought he was leaving to us would run out before his life ended.
All this transpired before long-term-care insurance was available.
I was grateful that Dad kept saying I could save the daily seventeen-
dollar cost by bringing him back to our house. If he only knew the
real charges!!

The Dad I knew, growing up and as an adult, was not there
anymore, and I was the only member of our immediate family left. I
so wished he was there to reminisce with. Once in a while a glimpse
of the old Dad would appear, and it felt wonderful. I'd forget that the
next sentence would usually be nonsensical. Living on this emotional
roller coaster takes a toll. I treasured the pictures the aides took of

him grinning in a bubble bath, or of him remembering the words and singing Christmas carols, even dancing with a nurse. The day came when his eyes glazed over, when his body was smaller than mine, when he didn't realize he was wearing diapers. He no longer asked to go home with me ... he no longer asked for anything. Many days I came and just fed him his meal and left. He slept a lot, and some days he resisted changing out of his clothes for pajamas at bedtime. The medications left him dopey, but he didn't push anybody.

One day I arrived and the nurse asked me who Papa was. Dad had walked into the dining room and exclaimed, "Why, Papa, what are you doing here?"

I'd heard that often a person who has preceded you in death comes as a spirit to help in your transition. Perhaps Dad's time was near. That night he didn't eat his supper and I knew we were near the end when the ice cream he loved just dribbled down his chin as I tried to entice him with his favorite chocolate. I kissed him goodnight as he reclined in a chair in the living room. When the midnight phone call announced his passing, I almost felt relieved. I sat up in bed and heard a tapping on the sliding door in our bedroom. Rising, I couldn't see anyone or anything outside. Somehow, I knew Dad was telling me he was free and alive once more.

MY NAME IS EARL

I am not referring to the television show, but our neighbor whose name is Earl. So many times my husband or I say, "Let's ask Earl, he'll know." And he does.

For many years my parents said, "Let's ask Betsy, she'll know." So I got to thinking about helpers in our lives. Do you have someone in your life that you turn to for assistance on a regular basis? Or, in this age of the internet, do we turn to it instead?

My spiritual community believes in looking within for answers. As a psychologist, I have found that people have their best wisdom within. People come to me for answers for life's decisions, and my job is to facilitate their finding the answer within. As an energy worker, I find that only we can remove blocks to our emotional, physical, or spiritual health. So, why and when *do* we ask the Earls in our lives?

It's the "how to" issues or "what's the best item for the task in front of us" that we look outside ourselves for the answers. It takes time to research answers to these questions and, so, we ask others. They've already done the research. For so much in life, so has the internet. It's our inner landscape that no one else has researched. That's our job and, yet, we shy away from doing it. Do we not think we can succeed, or do we just not want to go there?

I turned the television to the Bay Hill golf tournament. Arnold Palmer told the interviewer that his father instilled confidence in his game, advising him to not copy the golf masters but to trust his own instincts. And look how he has succeeded.

We seem to be reluctant to trust ourselves, preferring to give our power to others. I have found that there is a still, small voice inside that speaks wisdom whenever I am quiet enough to hear it. Often it speaks to me during prayer or meditation or, perhaps, a dream; other times just in an urging toward one alternative over others. These times I lean one way and let a day or so pass and see if I am still standing firm with that answer, or whether it has fallen away to be replaced by another. Then the pathway seems to be smooth sailing. I often refer to these occurrences as "being in the flow." Wise spiritual writers have suggested that when the desire of our heart meets Spirit's intention for us, that there is a certainty felt.

I do believe that to know ourselves and to grow in wisdom and consciousness, we need to do our own work. However, there are limits to everything. I am not a wise pro, nor am I a computer techie, and for better or worse, I am waiting for Earl to finish his household chores and walk up the driveway to our house. My latest story is deliberately hiding in this computer. I've searched everywhere for it, so I NEED to ask Earl.

NO LACK OF
COURAGE AND DETERMINATION

Thomina stood on the railing of the ship and looked up at the Statue of Liberty and wondered what was ahead for her in this new country. Her young husband, Manely, had come to America from Greece four years ago and started a little restaurant in Clarksburg, West Virginia. He became lonely and returned to his native Greece to find a bride. His first Sunday in church, he looked around and spied the fifteen-year-old beauty who was to become his wife. Problem was, she had an older sister the parents said had to be married before they would give permission for Thomina to marry. Manely was dejected, but determined to return to America with his lovely Thomina. He enlisted in the Greek navy and returned two years later to the waiting Thomina. By then her older sister had become a Greek wife. It was scary to leave family and country to sail across the ocean to a new land, but Thomina had come to love Manely and this four-foot-eleven-inch woman had never lacked for courage and determination.

As the young couple went through immigration at Ellis Island, the American officer, unable to pronounce their names, wrote down Mike and Domna Kaites, and so they were called from then on. When their first son and daughter were babies, the plague hit the world and both children died. Domna cried with despair, alone with the Greek ladies in the church in town instead of her beloved mother and sister. Mike stoically said that they'd just have to have more children. They eventually had two more sons and two more daughters. Domna insisted that the children not continue to work in the restaurant after high school, but go to college. This woman, who had only completed the fourth grade in Greece, had seen the path to success in her new country and was determined to provide this opportunity for her children.

Tragedy and depression again became Domna's companion when her oldest girl developed Hodgkin's disease while in her early twenties. Mary had been a surrogate mother to her younger siblings, an accomplished pianist and business woman, and her eventual death left a mark on them all. The younger son later married and named his first born daughter, Mary.

Domna sent clothes and medicine to her family back in Greece during World War II. Whenever she and Mike returned for a visit, they were received with gratitude. Mike retired from the restaurant business, enjoyed his older son's success in the town's fine clothing store, and his younger son's success with a coal company in a neighboring state. Domna continued to walk to town each day, shop, greet the salespeople, and have lunch in the department store cafeteria. After Mike's death, she lived alone in the house where she and Mike had raised their family, and was always eager for visits to and from her children and grandchildren.

"I want to go to Greece one more time before I die," this eighty-five-year-old told my husband, her younger son, and me in August, 1984. We polled the siblings to see if anyone was in a position to take her, but they were busier than we, so feeling some urgency to go now, we wrote the cousins in Greece and booked our trip. Domna's breathing was labored as we traveled. But she made it with the help of a few wheelchairs along the way. Of course, she protested each time we ordered one for her. She insisted on shopping in the Plaka in Athens, had coffee in the outdoor cafes, and flew to the island of Chios, where she had been born, visited with all the relatives, and made some jewelry purchases in the family's store to bring back to her children and grandchildren.

We returned from our trip in early October. I created a photo album which told the story of her trip and she showed it to all in town who would look. She condescended to take a taxi to and from town, as her walking had become more labored. The phone calls increased to her children, now established in their own lives, to come back to town and live with her. After all, this was what children did in Greece. We brought her to our house for Thanksgiving. My husband and his sister didn't give in to her pleading to come back home, but they encouraged her to spend more time with them in their homes and with her son, who still lived in town. Despite her tears, Domna quietly smiled and was proud of their independence and determination.

After a Thanksgiving dinner, grandchildren around the table, we continued our custom of each speaking in turn of the past year's highlight and a hope for the future year, for which they welcomed the family's support. Domna was the last to speak. It was quiet and we didn't know whether she would choose to join in our tradition or not. Suddenly she burst out with, "I don't want to die yet."

She silenced us all until I said, "Well, okay."

We proceeded to clear the food and do the dishes. Our older daughter and she were sitting at the kitchen table drying silverware when I heard my daughter say, "Come quickly, I think there's something wrong with Domna." One look and my husband called 911. She never regained consciousness from that massive stroke.

Domna was to travel to yet another land. She left us with grateful hearts that we had made that one last trip to Greece, and for a life that had inspired her family to be as loving, courageous, and determined as she.

GETTING READY FOR CHEMO

The unthinkable happened. Our forty-seven-year-old daughter, Joedy, was told her breast lump was cancerous. There was no history of breast cancer on either side of the family and, yet, two days later the young woman oncologist at this specialized clinic in Honolulu where Joedy lived, performed a lumpectomy and sent some lymph nodes to the pathologist. One of the nodes had cancer, so twenty-three others were taken out in a second procedure.

I cried inside when I heard. Honolulu is "out there" in the Pacific, not some neighboring state; so far away when you want to hug a daughter. And, besides, a trip to Europe with four of our other children, which had been two years in the planning, was less than a week away. Conflict about where to be stretched my heart.

Our son-in-law, Mike, cancelled a summer teaching opportunity in Africa. Our daughter insisted that my husband and I proceed with the planned trip to Europe, and the "getting ready for chemo" began.

After much discussion as to what would give Joedy the best chance at long-term survival, it was decided to administer the chemo in four heavy-duty doses, twenty-one days apart. Of course, the exact schedule would depend upon whether her blood count could stay up high enough, and no infection occurred.

"You will definitely lose your hair," the doctor stated. This caused eight-year-old Lauren to burst into tears, as her mom's hair was long and thick. However, thirteen-year-old grandson Chris envisioned drawing on his mom's bald head with magic markers. Joedy scheduled an appointment for a short haircut, was fitted for her wig, and bought a hat. She donated the rest of her hair for a wig for another.

A plane reservation was made for two days after I returned from Europe and our daughter, cheerfully, reassured us that Mike could deal with her needs for the first treatment, and that I would be back for the, more critical, other three.

Information was passed on from so many of my friends. Nearly everyone had a story of someone, or themselves, who had endured chemo. We put Joedy on Unity's prayer list, the Village said prayers for her for the next thirty days, and many of us said daily affirmations for healing.

E-mails from Honolulu reminded me to bring favorite recipes, chocolate from Switzerland, special surprises, and some books for my daughter. Having these normal motherly things to do helped make the dreaded chemo days ahead seem more manageable somehow.

All during the trip I was preparing myself for what I had learned to do, energetically, with my hands when I was with her. I was hopeful that this, plus great love, would be helpful in flushing excess chemo out of Joedy's system, thus minimizing damage to other areas of her body. We received an e-mail saying that the first treatment had gone well and to enjoy our travels. Turned out, it wasn't exactly so, but that is what daughters say to mothers when they are so far away.

As we checked out of our hotel in Italy, the white-haired owner wished us well on our next stop. Something prompted me to tell her of our daughter's health challenge. I was startled as she pulled her blouse down to reveal a scarred breast with a missing chunk.

"Years ago, when I was forty-one-years-old," she stated, "I had a breast cancer removed, then chemo, and here I am!" she exclaimed, triumphantly. She helped me to further get ready for the challenges that the chemo would bring.

The trip ended, and I was finally in Hawaii. All my preparation had not prepared me for my first glimpse of Joedy with her missing hair. My smiling daughter looked like my balding son. The lack of hair to frame her white face caused my heart to break a bit.

Joedy had settled into a routine of going bald in the house and wearing the hat outside. The wig was just too hot. Our son-in-law had shaved his head in support and by the time I arrived, even Lauren was used to Mom. All she asked was that her mom put the hat on when friends came over to play. I realized that I and the family could see the change in her hair. So we focused on that. It was harder to understand the viciousness of the chemo on her insides.

A routine soon emerged. The first night after chemo we could eat out as a treat for the family. Then the queasy stomach forced Joedy to stay away from kitchen smells. For about a week she sipped Ensure, ate canned peaches, drank as much liquid a she could keep down, and gradually came out to sit at the table and share in the news of the day.

Then one of the family pets developed a tumor. The kids and Mike were busy in summer school, so I needed to accompany Joedy on the trip to the vet, in case the odors in the office or the driving were too hard for her.

After school, my daughter insisted on supervising the backyard burial of this little gerbil. Joedy dealt with the tears as only a mom could do. She also was the only one who could toast the grilled cheese sandwiches, just right, and trim the crusts off. I came to understand that if it wasn't like Mom had done it, it just wasn't right.

The veins in her hand complained as the doctor attempted to start the fourth chemo treatment. Last one, we all smilingly said. By now, the doctor's technicians, even the other patients, were good buddies. Joedy and one other female patient sat in two big Lazy Boy chairs with the chemo dripping, intravenously, into the chosen hand. With the other hand she could hold a magazine. I was offered tea or coffee and was seated nearby. This part of chemo treatment wasn't so bad. The warmth of the folks helped us forget that there was a real nasty attack being prepared for the days ahead. But this day, after the chemo, we went out to lunch, like mothers and daughters do.

That night, our grandson's dinner prayer was to thank the hands that had prepared the food, even though it wasn't like Mom would have done, and then he petitioned God to help Mom get well and that Joe, the runaway turtle, return. Losses were especially difficult those days.

We got used to Mom reading a lot in her room. It fell to me to help Lauren clean out her closet, drawers, and desk in readiness for the beginning of school. I was even pressed into service to carry Chris's rocket launcher to the park one afternoon.

Soon Joedy could come out to the living room after supper and join the family for movie night with popcorn and juice. Some nights were game nights and it was heart warming to see my daughter's joy at being the mom of this family. Being there for these months gave me a chance to know that my granddaughter aspired to be a "bunny breeder" and my grandson some kind of a rocket engineer. The closeness we developed was something that just doesn't happen on the briefer family visits.

Cousins from the mainland were due to arrive for the annual shared vacation trip to the Big Island. With my help, we all were able to go on this "normal" family outing. It was fun for me to see the kids interact and to share in a special family time together.

It was now time for me to leave and let the family manage on their own once again. We had survived the worst that chemo could do and had faith that it accomplished its good work. I kissed them good-bye, filled with gratitude for this family and its love and support for each other. I know because of her good treatment, prayers of so many, and her positive attitude, that she will live to have white hair like the woman in Italy.

And because of all that, I was able to get beyond chemo's challenges and return home with the blessings that special sharing and loving time together gifted us with.

MOO AND ME REVISITED

Had twenty-three years really passed since our first grandchild was born? We drove from Arizona to California and, with our daughter, sat on the bleachers of San Jose State University where Nick was granted a diploma. Following the lengthy ceremony, he was eager to take off the newly acquired cap and gown and replace them with the more familiar jeans and tee shirt. We followed him to the apartment he shared with two other guys and a cat named Rascal. As he petted his furry friend his mother smiled in remembrance of his first animal friend, Moo.

Nick grinned, commenting that he had dearly loved that stuffed cow.

Returning to compile stories for this collection, I was reminded of an article I had written for the Town of Paradise Valley's independent newspaper twenty years ago when I wrote a weekly column. I decided to include it:

Nicholas, our twenty-month-old grandson, came to visit this week-end and brought his best friend, Moo. It seems to be genetic, this independent trait he exhibits. Nicholas has several more 'usual' stuffed animals: teddy bears, dogs, kittens, and rabbits. But what does he choose to love? A stuffed cow he calls Moo.

His first day here we went to the zoo. It's interesting that one of the first things we do with young children is to introduce them to animals. My father still asks if I remember the balloons tied to my stroller and the ice-cream cone we'd get on our way home from the every-Sunday afternoon visit to the Baltimore Zoo. He'll never know whether I remember or not, but I know I've always loved and lived with animals. Mom recently gave me a little picture scrapbook I'd made as a child entitled, *My Fourteen Cats*. I also had six dogs. I still have a dog, and my grandchildren all have animals.

Studies show children raised with animals (where there is love and responsibility required in their care) become loving and responsible adults. I've seen the healing effect of animals brought into nursing homes, retirement homes, and rehab centers. Our dog, Chablis, brought a smile to my dad's face when he had Alzheimer's when nothing else could.

My children learned much about the birds and bees when our pet goat, April, was brought into our family room and gave birth to three kids. I can still see our twelve-year-old son giving a bottle to the "runt," who would later follow him on hikes through the woods like a pet dog.

Our children are no longer at home, so we don't have the school activities or their friends to facilitate easy introduction to neighbors. Walking my dog each day has let me meet Buffy's owner, Duke's family, Tabby the cat's folks, and other neighbors with animal pets.

Sunday afternoon we took Nicholas to the McCormick Railroad Park for a ride on the new carousel. His little eyes were big as the gaily painted horses went up and down. When the music ground down and the carved horse stopped moving, we took Nicholas off his mount. I can still hear his pleading voice, "My horsey, my horsey .... more."

We returned him to his stroller where his thumb silenced his tears. He had no use for us – only Moo.

Nicholas's mother carried him past the departure gate at Sky Harbor International Airport on his way home to Denver. His one little hand waved bye-bye, the other clutched Moo.

Twenty years later, I believe that Moo did what he came into this world to do. Nicholas is a loving, respectful, and responsible young man. After returning home, I attended a service at Unity and picked up one of the stuffed critters on the pew chair. These animals sit for a year and soak up loving hugs until Christmas when the choir carols and leaves them to bless a shut-in or nursing home resident. Out of curiosity I looked around the church after the service, but I didn't see a stuffed cow anywhere. I guess there was just one Moo.

THERE'S SOMETHING
ABOUT A MOTHER'S LOVE

My daughter, Laurie, called to talk about her baby's baptism. What to wear, how much to pay the minister, and how to celebrate the day. I thought back to the day she was baptized. It was a big day for me, but no big deal to her dad. This triggered my thoughts about important times in our children's lives and the different responses of men and women.

Why is it that the smallest details of a mother's relationship with her child are more delicious when shared with someone who understands, like her own mother? Somehow in the sharing and the mutual joy, the moment is intensified; the relationship closer and deepened.

Is this the same for Mother God? Does she love to share in the joys of our lives; the birth of new puppies; the laughter of a child splashing in a puddle; pride during walks across stages at graduation?

Do fathers want to share aspects of child-rearing with another? Details of a baptism, a prom or even a wedding are not usually shared and relived with another man. My son's calls are more about trophies won, bones broken, mountains climbed.

Perhaps it is only that women's hearts expand with these loving moments and that men are from Mars. What makes the sharing of the Venus feelings special? There is a bonding that is often present between close women friends and their children's slights and triumphs, one that wasn't there between my daughters and me before the commonality of motherhood in my daughters' lives.

What is this common thread? Shared experience? If we are all one, why are usually the mothers' hearts connected in understanding? And why is it not true for all mothers and daughters? Are those who share this appreciation on the same *consciousness* level rather than the same gender?

Some might say this phenomenon is as simple as common interests. But, somehow, I don't think so. I just know that I am feeling blessed that a daughter's new motherhood has brought us closer, that my female friends relate and smile with happiness for me, and that there is already a special feeling for this new granddaughter.

I know that my grandmother and I had a special connection that my mother, with her differences, did not. But maybe Grandmother just had a more relaxed time to focus on me. I think I missed out on a deeper closeness with my mother by not stretching my boundaries or comfort zone. As I age, there are memories of Mother's life that I could more easily share now and I miss her. At times I sense my older daughter sees the bond between her daughter and me as easy, while hers is a more difficult one. Grandmothers often can just focus on the good stuff!

I don't notice most men dwelling on matters of the heart like this. Their more developed left brains focus on the concrete. "Did she say when she'd return home with the car?" ... "What are the details of her new job offer?" ... "What about the company's benefits?" ... "Do you want to go to the game with me or not?" ... "When do we eat?"

Men seem to bond over work, athletics, and business deals. My retiree husband often yearns for other men to participate in our church study groups which focus on spiritual growth. Does it take serious loss for a man to turn more inward to his heart? We do see men at Deepak Chopra's study group; however, Deepak often writes about energy and more scientific subjects.

We have learned that division of labor started in the early times when women stayed by the fireside, cooking and minding the children while men hunted for food. History has educated us all of our different roles in life. In today's world, however, more and more women are in the more left-brained occupations. Is it possible that today we can appreciate our gender differences and also experience common strivings for purposeful lives, and meaningful times of sharing?

So, I am back to my musings, and what is it about a mother's heart? At the moment, it is special to share the depth of feelings and meaning of a baby girl's baptism with a daughter.

STEPHEN AND THE KING OF SIAM

I found two unique scraps of paper stuck into a book of family genealogy. My mother, Helen Mattoon, was always proud of her ancestry. As a young person, stories of my relatives' exploits never seemed as important to me as what each family member was doing with his life in the present. The past met the present the other day as I picked up the papers, recognized her handwriting, and was lured to continue reading.

My great-great-grandfather and his family, proud Huguenots, escaped persecution for their Protestant beliefs in France and immigrated to the United States. Stephen Mattoon attended Princeton University where he obtained a teaching certificate and then went on to Union where he obtained a ministerial degree. After he and Mary were married, they departed for Siam in 1847, where they served as pioneer missionaries for the Presbyterian Church for the next twenty years.

During negotiations of a new treaty between Siam and the British

Empire, King Mongkut chose Stephen to be his interpreter. When consular relations with the United States were established, Stephen Mattoon was appointed the first consul. He remained at that post only a short time, as his first love was missionary work.

In 1851, King Mongkut invited Mary Mattoon and two other American women into the forbidden area of the Palace to teach the women of his household. Shortly afterward, Mary Mattoon urged King Mongkut to employ a full-time teacher for the princes and their wives. This suggestion eventually led to the arrival in Siam of Anna Leonowens, later immortalized in *Anna and the King of Siam*.

In 1866, after translating the Bible into Siamese, Stephen and Mary Mattoon returned to the United States where he became pastor of a Presbyterian church in a town near Sarasota, New York. In 1870, Stephen became the first regular president of a Presbyterian college for Negroes in Charlotte, North Carolina, now Johnson C. Smith University.

Our family is Presbyterian and I have been active in the church, serving as a lay minister. I attended Oberlin College, the first in the United States to admit African Americans. Oberlin was at the Northern end of the Underground Railroad during the Civil War days. I have a passion for travel in my bones and a love of service to others. Guess I come by these honestly.

I was proud to read of Stephen Mattoon and was startled to recall my mother's question as to why I chose to name a son Stephen when no one in the family had that name. "I just like it," I had replied.

I smiled and wished Mother were alive to share my discovery of her story written on scraps of paper many years ago. I wish she were alive to know how the teachings of her grandson, Stephen, impacts the lives of youth in his small community. But I can share it with you, and somehow I feel like Paul Harvey when he says, "and now you know the rest of the story."

Part Two:
Voices of Other Cultures

A Visit with Mother Teresa

She was found wherever there was need, this bent and wrinkled seventy-six-year-old living saint of Calcutta, the winner of a 1979 Nobel Prize. Our delegation from the United States, studying women's issues in India, had just arrived January 19, 1989, at the main headquarters of the Missionaries of Charity.

We had passed through the crowds of five-hundred street people gathered outside the gate, waiting for a bowl of rice. We saw the eighty children, ill from tuberculosis or infection, brought to the center for medical care by their families or identified by the sisters during their daily home visits. We saw the one-hundred-thirty children, ages one to three, who were eligible for adoption, and the fifteen mentally handicapped children who will stay at the center until they die.

The clean interior of the building contrasted with the dust and grime of the street and the tattered attire of the street people. Inside, the attendants wore crisp, navy and white dresses with white pointy caps that kept their hair neat.

The possibility of meeting Mother Teresa was the strongest emotional pull in my decision to be a part of this People-to-People Citizen Ambassador trip. Responding to people's needs whenever and wherever she found them, this living saint would make no commitment to our delegation leader, Sham Dudoni, as to whether she would be in Calcutta at the time of our visit and whether she would be able to meet with us. I had all my fingers crossed in the hope that no emergency or need would appear to take her away from us that day. As we rounded a corner inside the building, I heard a startled gasp from one of our delegation.

"Oh, my God, there she is!" Around the corner came this tiny, aged nun, shrouded in a blue shawl, radiating her way towards us.

Mother Teresa was born in Albania in 1910 of well-to-do parents. She wrote that she always knew she was to help the poor and by 1931 had emigrated to Calcutta as a high school teacher. Her "call" was to serve God by living among the poor, so she began by witnessing a basic need and addressing it. The people she assisted, then the wider community and, soon, donors, observed her good works and started helping her. And so it went over the years. By 1989, there were three-thousand sisters and four-hundred brothers of her missionary order feeding one-hundred-thirty-six-thousand families, teaching fourteen-thousand children in ninety-seven schools, caring for one-hundred-eighty-six-thousand victims of leprosy, and twenty-two-thousand dying destitute.

Mother Teresa asked the purpose of our visit to India. Barbara, a television interviewer, told her of our interest in the challenges Indian women faced as they became more liberated. We wanted to learn of her journey and success in responding to the needs of the poor in India. Sham had told us that she had refused to meet with a Japanese delegation the day before because they seemed more interested in meeting the famous Mother Teresa than the people she served. They left their sizable donation and had to leave.

Sham had wisely taken us to the orphanage and the kitchens preparing rice for the beggars outside the gates before climbing the stairs to the administration wing. Mother Teresa spoke to us because we were interested in her work. We dialogued about the Missionaries of Charity centers in America, our countrys' options for unwed mothers, and adoption policies.

As we readied to leave, our spokeswoman asked if she had any message we could take back to the women in our country. Hanging on every word, we strained to hear the five-word quote from Jesus, "You do it unto me."

She went on to encourage us to do all we could, wherever we came from, to feed the hungry, clothe the naked, care for the children, and know that we were doing God's work. As she turned to leave, she glanced back at us and added, "And remember, the family that prays together, stays together."

More memorable than her words was the energy and light emanating from this tiny powerhouse. I had never experienced anything like air so thick it was palpable, electricity in my hands, and an overwhelming feeling of peace and love. I sensed that I had opened up to a deeper awareness of myself due to being so intensely in the NOW.

We were all absorbed with our own thoughts as the bus pulled away from the Mission. Back at the hotel, we gathered to speak of how this woman had followed her inner guidance and acted upon what had brought such passionate feeling to her. Each of us, accomplished in our fields, looked inside our hearts to our dreams, desires, and passions, and challenged ourselves as to whether we were fulfilling them.

I vowed to follow my interest in infusing my counseling with energy healing and to give slide presentations to groups in the Phoenix community regarding the dialogues we had experienced in India. The doctor, affected by the increased healing love generated by families staying on the hospital grounds until their loved one was released, vowed to encourage a less sterile environment, while a retirement officer promised to look into offering more assistance in keeping the elderly in their homes longer. A company executive planned to fight harder to locate employees nearer their extended families and a television executive promised to feature inspirational interviews like

Mother Teresa's.

We came to see the work of a saint. We left challenging ourselves as to how we could more fully be the hands of God in our lives when we returned to our land from hers.

THE PRIEST

The only other passenger on the train asked if we were going to Todi, a hilltop town in Italy. We told him that we were going there to visit our son, an art professor at Penn State, who was teaching drawing to his college students during a seven-week program. As we left Assisi, the noise of the train resembled a passenger car changing gears; our puzzled looks caught the attention of the conductor, who explained that we were riding in a diesel engine train.

Our traveling companion informed us that he was on his way to a small town seven miles from Todi, a town in which an International Assembly of Catholic Bishops was scheduled during the following week. This man said he planned to walk the distance between Todi and the town since he couldn't find public transportation, and on his meager salary he couldn't afford a taxi. He had the brightest smile and his eyes crinkled with love and eagerness. The entire car seemed to fill with his warmth.

In response to our interest, he reported that he was going to the Assembly to locate the bishop who would ordain him. He grinned and said that no one would ordain him in his native Germany.

The conductor, all dressed in his official uniform, returned with a broad smile and was pleased to tell our German friend that the driver had agreed to make a special stop for him to get off at the town. He gratefully responded, "Only in Italy."

Looking out the window, I saw the magnificent fields of wheat and green pastures, but they were not as interesting to me as this plain man with the wonderful energy riding in our car. All kinds of reasons for the difficulty in his becoming ordained went through my head. Possibly he was gay; after all, he was in mid-life, slender, slightly effeminate, and probably without family attachments.

Maybe his previous career ended in disgrace, or even something dark and sinister in his past caused the ever more cautious Catholic Church to be afraid of yet another priest scandal. I couldn't remain silent any longer. I arose, approached him, and apologized if my question was intrusive.

"Why," I asked, "wouldn't they ordain you in Germany?"

"Oh," he smiled and replied, "They find me too spiritual."

The man went on to share his more contemporary beliefs, which included energy, mediumship, New Thought theology, and healing ... all thinking I agreed with. I excitedly told him of my studies with Reverend Rosalyn L. Bruyere of California, an energy teacher and extraordinary healer. Also, that our Unity Church in the States was full of "recovered Catholics" who were drawn to a church community who believed in the New Thought theology that Charles and Myrtle Fillmore had written about. We soon exchanged e-mail addresses. My husband came over to share that he had gone into meditation and had visualized the man's ordination.

"Oh, yes! A German psychic had also seen me being ordained, and by a bishop who would be attending this gathering in Italy; and that's why I'm here."

We all agreed to pray for Divine Order and acknowledged with gratitude that it would happen.

The train slowed, its brakes squealed, and the man quickly gathered his belongings. A whistle blew and the conductor arrived, announcing that this was the place. With a confident smile and a light step, the soon-to-be priest swung off the train. He waved at us as the toy-like train started to roll along the tracks toward Todi. We looked out the windows at the peaceful, green countryside with cypress trees lining the driveways of the sporadic farmhouses. There were no towns to be seen.

Our son met us at the train station and inquired about our ride.

"Just us and a priest," we answered, with grins.

PICK-POCKETED IN PRAGUE

As seasoned travelers, my husband and I understand there's a certain amount of risk traveling abroad. We always envision a "shield of protection" around us when we go on a trip. Once, that visualization failed us.

It happened when we were traveling with a group of family members on a Danube River cruise to celebrate John's eightieth birthday. On the first morning of the tour, a magnificent vista of spires beckoned from our Prague hotel room. We dressed quickly, eager to enjoy the ambience of this European city. Our daughter had suggested taking a streetcar to the old city and walking across the historic Charles Bridge for our first excursion, and we agreed.

We set out after breakfast, walking the cobblestoned streets toward the streetcar stop. A young couple was already waiting, and they reassured us that we were at the right stop to head to town. Soon enough, a red streetcar creaked to a halt in front of us, and two sets of doors opened. Our daughter and her friend mounted the front two steps while my husband and I waited behind the young couple at the second door. We were suddenly conscious of several young adults pushing behind us. I heard my husband yell, "Hey, get away from me," and when I turned toward him, he exclaimed, "They got my wallet!"

The people ahead of us dispersed to allow our daughter and her friend to get off the car. No one in the streetcar reacted, so I ran toward the streetcar station yelling, "Police!" The streetcar closed its doors and continued its path toward town.

When I walked back to the group, John was insisting that our daughter and her friend continue with their plans to sightsee, and they reluctantly agreed. The two of us returned to the hotel to report the theft, all the while my husband ranting, "Where were the police?" and, "If Prague is known for pickpockets, why weren't there any police at the station?"

The clerk was sympathetic and gave us a theft report form to complete while she dialed the station to report our loss. Of course, the police would return the wallet, credit card, and driver's license if they found them. Yes, they would send them on to the next stop on our tour. And, here is the number for the U.S. Visa office to cancel our card. We returned to our room, John still fuming and I quiet.

I didn't want to venture out alone, nor stay in the room with my moody husband, so I put on my bathing suit and left for the hotel pool. What a wretched beginning to our much-anticipated trip.

After swimming out my frustrations, I cautiously returned to the room. John was seated in a chair. With a smile on his face, he pronounced, "I have just had the most marvelous experience." Looking for the open wine bottle and seeing none, I asked him to say more.

"Well, I went into meditation," he explained, "and this voice clearly said, 'Love them. Love them, for they know not what they do.'"

He went on: "I first said, 'fuck them,' out loud. Then I clearly heard again, 'Love them.' There was a complete shift in me," he said. "I went from remunerating about what had happened to me, which was head stuff, into my heart. I have been sitting here sending them love, forgiving them, and I feel great!"

I couldn't believe my ears. I had been fearful that this event would ruin our dinner celebration, if not the entire trip. Instead, John had transformed his anger into an opportunity to send love to the pick-pocketers and, hopefully, affect them positively.

Feeling fortunate to have only lost one credit card and eighty dollars, we took off for the city center once more. Of course, I gripped my purse tightly and my husband had no wallet to secure, but the day was brighter than before.

When we met up with the others, John told of his meditation and how the voice had transformed his emotions. He asked for our prayers for the pick-pocketers, and I gave an extra prayer of gratitude for John's choice to be a loving person in Prague in his dealing with his challenge.

LORENZA'S WAY

While driving up the roadway that wound through two-thousand acres of vineyards and age-old pines in the Tuscan area of Guioli, Italy, I wondered what Lorenza de Medici would be like. The one-thousand-year-old former Benedictine monastery came into view as our driver rounded the last curve. This villa, Badia, a Coltibuono Abbey of the Good Hearth, was now owned by Lorenza's husband, of the Stucchi Prinetti family. Piero's inheritance was to be our home for the next five days.

My friend, Carolyn, and I were there for one of the few cooking classes Lorenza gave each year. Imagine my delight at receiving a letter from my former college roommate stating that she had signed us both up for the October 8th class! I was to be at the Excelsior Hotel, in Florence, Italy, at 3:00pm. A van would drive us to The Villa Table. Carolyn and I had studied about the great de Medici family while students at Oberlin College years before. We both had developed an appreciation of Italian cuisine in the years since, but to go to this most prestigious wine estate in the heart of the Chianti Classico Tuscan hills was more than a dream. Carolyn, whose aunt had left her some money (which she used to fund our trip), told me that in addition to the participation in the cooking classes, there would be excursions into the cultural life of the region, and evening dinners in nearby private castles, villas, and beautiful homes of Lorenza's friends.

Lorenza, a lovely woman with sparkling eyes and quick movements, greeted us in the drawing room, which was dominated by a sixteenth-century fresco. Wine from the Coltibuono vineyards was served by a young, sleek man from Sri Lanka. Lorenza had rescued him from an alcoholic, depressed, poverty-stricken life while on a trip to his country. She hired him to be a valet for her husband, Piero, who had recently suffered a stroke.

There were sixteen of us in the room, all Americans eager to experience modern-day Italian aristocracy, with the added prospect of enriching our lives with gourmet recipes. Lorenza moved easily among the new students: a New York trial lawyer and his wife; Linda Gray, the Hollywood actress turned Good-Will Ambassador, who had played J.R.'s wife on the television show, *Dallas*; a company CEO and his wife, on their honeymoon; a lawyer for Sprint; a housewife whose husband had given her the trip as a gift; and Carolyn and me.

We soon settled into our private guest rooms, located along the grand fifteenth-century corridor of the upper floor, with its heavy wooden-beamed ceiling and sixteenth-century frescos.

Mornings began with us sitting around her large dining room table, covered with a linoleum cloth to protect it from the pen marks we made on our daily recipes.

Lorenza talked about the dishes which we were to prepare for lunch. They expressed her approach to cooking: personal, simple, elegant, and with many ingredients coming from her own large kitchen garden. She told stories about her four children, now adults, and each in charge of one aspect of the working estate. While teenagers, her boys loaded the car with "herbs" from the garden, ready to go to Sienna. One of the employees came to Lorenza to make sure she approved of the boys taking marijuana in to the city to sell! That was the end of that garden "herb." Stories like these made the ocean that separates our countries seem small or non-existent.

After the discussion, we grabbed our recipes and followed her into the well-equipped kitchen. We sat on bar stools on one side of the work counter while Lorenza and her assistant, the young Bosnian wife of the valet, started the menu on the other side of the counter. Such fun we had! Lorenza's charm was her naturalness. No airs, no attempt to make good cuisine complicated.

We students chopped herbs with a mezzaluna, a sickle shaped knife, incorporated eggs into a flour bowl with a fork, and always used hands to separate the eggs.

"Your hands are your best kitchen tools," Lorenza said with a smile. "You Americans have way too many kitchen accessories."

Piero always joined us in the dining room for the 1:00pm meal that we had prepared, and Lorenza sat next to him at the head of the table. He had had three strokes and hardly spoke, but the dashing Italian eyes told their own stories.

As he flirted with the actress, Lorenza said, "You Americans ... you were so silly over Monica. Men have hundreds of lovers." Not one of us doubted that she had shrugged and accepted this as the way it was in her life.

There were always the best wines from their vineyard. As the meal progressed, Lorenza told us of growing up as a member of the well-educated, cultured elite in Northern Italy. The dashing Piero courted her, they married, and then she raised their four children while he traveled, marketed, and developed the estate into the success it is today. The family exports one million bottles of Chianti Classico and Vin Santo wines, plus harvesting olives, exporting olive oil, vinegars, honey, and soaps. Each of Piero and Lorenza's adult children, all educated in the United States, was in charge of one aspect of the enterprise.

We met one son who operated a fine restaurant on the property and were treated to a boar's head luncheon on our last day there. Another son was in charge of the vineyard and we had a wine tasting one afternoon. The daughter, in charge of marketing, was in New York.

We all had free time in the afternoon before meeting John, Lorenza's trusted friend and the driver, at 4:30pm for our tour into the country-side and a visit and dinner at one of the castles or villas. The main chef at the Red Baron's estate recognized our Hollywood actress and we were treated royally and had a grand tour of the estate. Somehow the world seemed smaller and we became closer realizing that we all watched the same television shows.

Lorenza told us that this was the last year she would do the cooking school. These days, she goes to the opera in Milan with friends, travels to New York with her daughter and granddaughter, and has a full life. Thanks to Linda Gray's boyfriend, who was a composer, we presented Lorenza with this song as she gave us our diplomas:

LORENZA'S WAY
(to the tune of Sinatra's *My Way*)

And now, our school is done,
Our cooking classes all have ended.
I've learned Lorenza's rules and not a one can be suspended.
Recall each treasured phrase
At the start and end of days.
And more, much more than this,
You'll know Lorenza's Ways.

For what is a salad?
What does it mean?
If you put carrots in salad greens?
And if risotto you would munch
You serve it only just at lunch!
It is clear as night and day
It is Lorenza's Way.

Meat balls and microwaves
These are two things that are verboten,

Like plates that are pre-arranged
Or jello molds, these go unspoken.
I could ignore all of these
And like a fool spend the days,
But no, I've been to school
I've learned Lorenza's Ways.

For what is pasta in a pot?
If it has oil, you eat it not!
And here is lesson number two
Unless it boils, it tastes like glue.
The record shows
Lorenza knows.
These are Lorenza's Ways.

DEEPA'S LIFE, GROWTH, AND HOPE

She said her name was Deepa. "I will be your guide in Delhi," she announced to the fifty-five professionals who were citizen ambassadors on the People-to-People delegation to India and Nepal in 1988.

We were there to learn about women and their concerns, and to share our Western experiences with them. We heard presentations about women's issues from speakers in every field, but I learned about Indian women from Deepa. She listened quietly during our meetings, only talking when she was in charge of the tour. That is, until we went on a four-hour bus trip to Agra to see the Taj Mahal, and she talked to me about her life.

Deepa, the daughter of a diplomat, and her sister were born in Brazil and attended school in France before returning to the family home in what is now Pakistan. After the partition that separated India from Pakistan became official, the family fled to India without their possessions.

When Deepa was eighteen years old, her father set about arranging her marriage. Since in India you marry a family, not a man, he looked for one with similar educational and economic status. He presented Deepa with a young man of twenty-two, and she could say yes or no. Like most in those days, she agreed, and her subjugation shifted from her father to her husband.

The morning after their marriage, Deepa was given a diamond to place in her pierced left nostril. She had worn a round ring in her nose to signify virginity since age three. Newly married, she also wore silver ankle bracelets, which announced her presence and desire to speak. If her mother-in-law consented, Deepa could communicate to her husband by addressing him as "Mister." One of the recent changes she had made in her life was to call her husband by his initials, R.K., and to take off her silver shackles.

Deepa had two sons, ages eleven and fourteen. Since males are valued, share every avenue to power and opportunity in Indian society, can acquire, own, and transfer property, plus receive education, Deepa was not only honored by her husband for bearing sons, but they could look forward to a prosperous life. They did not have to save for a dowry, their future in-laws would not only provide them, but give them gifts for each holiday. Their culture was reflected in the theft of new mothers' infant sons in Delhi for sale in the black market, or the substitution in hospitals of baby boys for girls. Ninety-nine percent of abortions in India were for baby girls.

When her sons were in school, her parents and sister in England, and her days filled with housework under her mother-in-law's direction, Deepa was told of a job opening for a person who could speak French. Pleased with the prospect of additional income, R.K. allowed Deepa to take the qualifying exam and then the training. When her new job required an overnight stay in Agra, both her husband and her mother-in-law said no. Deepa closed her eyes as she recalled her decision to risk divorce for refusing to quit her job. I marveled at her courage.

We arrived in Agra at the Taj Mahal. This fragile, beautiful, yet massive monument to a man's love for his dead wife loomed in front of the long reflecting pools of water. The white marble took on a pink Valentine glow in the setting sunlight.

As I sat on a marble bench gazing in wonder at this tribute to a woman in this land that devalues women, I thought of Deepa's words, "In India, first comes marriage, then love."

Revisiting this trip, I took my eyes off my computer, gazed out my Arizona mountain window, and wondered what growth and hope had come to women in India in the twenty years since I rode on that bus with a woman named Deepa.

OUT OF THIS WORLD

Rev. Harry anointed my wrist with his special bottled essence. "This will help us have a spiritual experience somewhere on our trip," he stated convincingly.

We were on a tour entitled, *In the Footsteps of St. Paul*, going to Greece and Turkey. Harry was the youngest member of our group of eighteen, and the only minister. I was excited to be walking in St. Paul's footsteps and wondered whether my spiritual experience would be at Mars Hill, in Athens, where Paul spoke to the pagans; Corinth where he spoke and we planned to have a communion service; or, perhaps, in Ephesus, the home of the Virgin Mary.

Harry jogged each morning and I would get up early to practice my Chi Gong exercises. We kept checking with each other to see if the special experience had occurred for either one of us.

"Not yet," was our expectant reply.

Aware that scent shifts consciousness, I put on my essential oil for each day ahead. This particular day's plan seemed less interesting to me. We were in Turkey and on the long bus trip from Ephesus to Troy, with a stop set for Gallipoli, the site of a tragic World War I campaign, a joint British Empire and French operation mounted to capture the Ottoman capital of Constantinople and secure a sea route to Russia. The failed campaign lasted from April, 1915, through January, 1916, with heavy casualties on both sides.

The Gallipoli campaign began in the early 1900s when a ship of brave young New Zealand and Australian soldiers deployed on the Gallipoli peninsula beachfront, ready to face the Turks. The Turks fought under the fiercest warrior of the day, Atiturk, whose goal was to conquer the known world.

A statue of Atiturk stood on the hill overlooking the beach, seeming to mock us as we departed our bus. Our guide started his spiel by saying that all the soldiers had been massacred as they left their ship and waded ashore. The Turkish army, protected by trees on the high hill above, picked off the young Aussies and New Zealanders, one by one.

I went down to the beach and, as I walked, sensed the presence of others. I looked around and no one was there. The group had gone up the hill to look at the statue. I thought I heard moans, groans, and cries and I felt in the presence of souls, young souls, young soldiers still here, lost in this world.

I had learned from my energy teacher, Rosalyn Bruyere, how to visualize a column to let lost souls ascend to the spirit world. Rosalyn and others did this in New York after 9/11.

It felt right to perform this visualization that day on that beach in Gallipoli, Turkey. I often think of this vivid experience, certainly not the spiritual inspiration I expected, but the one that was right for me that day. Without Harry's essence, I might not have been open enough to hear the call and help free those tortured souls to leave that war-torn beach and ascend from this world.

A LOMI-LOMI

How do you decide whether to have a two-hour or a four-hour Lomi-Lomi? He'll tell you what you need, I was told. That's all well and good, but the appointment had to be scheduled from the mainland at least a month before seeing him. So, I scheduled a two-hour session for my husband and me with this internationally acclaimed body-worker/healer in Kauai.

A friend challenged me with the comment, "How often will you get the opportunity to have a Lomi-Lomi? Take the four-hour session!"

So, I called back only to learn that he was totally booked, and I'd have to settle for the two-hour massage-like Hawaiian treatment.

It was the day before our scheduled session. We were basking in the sunshine at our time-share resort in Princeville, watching the waves break in the surf outside, not a care in our world, when the phone rang. Alan's wife asked if I could come a day later as Alan had an emergency at my scheduled time.

"However," she added, "he can give you a four-hour appointment the next day."

It was meant to be.

We drove the two and a half miles along a pot-hole ridden, single-lane dirt road between fields of taro alongside a river in Hanalei. It was the land of Puff the Magic Dragon, and I wondered what kind of magic we expected from this Lomi-Lomi man.

At the end of the lane, we came up to the chain we were told would be across the road. Thick bamboo separated the road from Alan's green wooden house. As we approached the little house, we saw a metal washtub containing eight newborn puppies, and the mother protectively hovering nearby. Alan greeted us and I left my husband at the door and drove back out the road to the town of Hanalai to do touristy things.

The art exhibit I found was colorful with paintings of fish, flowers, and the ocean. I browsed through a gift shop, and at the local market selected some fresh fish for dinner. All the while I wondered what was going on with the Lomi-Lomi.

Two hours later, I retraced my path and parked outside to wait for my husband. Two hours became three. They finally came out and I saw this stocky man, arm in arm with John. My husband's eyes looked different, and Alan announced that John's little boy was healed and he had experienced a significant time. John gave me a funny smile and looked like he was still in an altered state. Then hugs all around and Alan looked deeply into my eyes and said he would see me the next day.

"Well, tell me about it," I eagerly asked. Just like a husband, he deferred, saying I would have my own experience and then we'd talk.

Morning came. I again drove down the dirt road, eager for my time with Alan. Not interested in shopping, John stayed at the hotel. I hopped up on the massage table, my underwear-clad body under the sheet. I asked this forty-one-year-old man when he had begun doing treatments.

"My grandmother recognized my gift when I was six, blindfolded me, and had me work on her daily for a month. I learned to listen to my hands, and to feel nuances in her body. I was allowed to begin doing treatments at age ten."

This gift had been passed down for at least six generations in his family. Alan said he had not done healing full time until his grandmother passed at age ninety-two. "Now, I travel all over the world, as well as give treatments at home."

He began. His hands went to the places in my body where I had stored emotions. I felt knots in certain back muscles and he rubbed them out. We talked about me and the messages he was getting about my stored emotions. He shared some wisdom about life and the daily schedule that best suits our bodies.

"Awake with the sun, meditate and bless the day, exercise, and then have breakfast. I walk for an hour after eating breakfast, work, have lunch, and then take a nap. I return to work until time to exercise again, play, and eat dinner. Bedtime is about 8:00pm."

He went on to add that during the first two hours of sleep the body replenishes the immune system. The next two hours the muscles get attention and then REM sleep, when our dreaming is in touch with our subconscious.

"So," he said, "we are as God created us to be ... happy, playful, joyful, and attuned to each other in the flow of life that is our individual manifestation of the God energy."

"Ouch!!!" Our conversation was interrupted by a blockage my body had developed due to a negative feeling.

Alan smoothed the knot, restored the energy flow and said that that part of my body, which had been fear, anger, or sadness, was now like it was when I was a baby girl.

Each evening, he told me, his family joins hands, prays, sings, and shares the best thing that happened in each of their lives that day.

"Positive energy begets goodness and blessings," he stated. "We do not need counselor's here," he laughingly said, knowing that I was a counselor on the mainland.

"You know, it's strange," he reflected, "I see many psychotherapists like you. Most have energy blocks in their bodies. The knots block energy and make the heart pump harder to get the blood through."

I told him of the statistic about psychiatrists dying at young ages. He commented that my pelvis was tilted and my back uneven and I told him of my life-long back problems.

"Yes, I know," was his compassionate reply. More massaging and then he remarked that my body was telling him of some previous kidney problem.

I laughingly told him that when I attended an intense twelve-day workshop with his friend, Dr. Brugh Joy, Brugh had suggested that we each take at least a day to reflect and integrate our learning and re-adjust to our lives when leaving the workshop. However, I had clients scheduled and had already taken a lot of time off, so was headed straight for the office. On the way home, I experienced intense pain and went directly to the hospital only to spend days waiting for the kidney stone to pass. My body knew I needed time to integrate the workshop and gave me the opportunity to do just that. Such needless suffering to give me a lesson about my choice!

Alan told me his grandmother said, "People come to body workers IF they believe the body stores memories and is part of the way we gain wisdom, and WHEN they are ready to live life more consciously."

Alan's eyes twinkled as he remarked that he wasn't saying anything that I didn't already know, just that I had stuff covered up that needed released. He gave me the homework of going out and playing in my world.

"We can be of service only when we are balanced physically, mentally, and spiritually."

How many times had I said that to others!!!

"Ouch!" Another sore spot, probably from too much giving and carrying responsibility for others. Alan suggested that I spend some time each day in my baby girl state and play, deal with negatives when they come, and are new, so that energy flows. It's called living more fully in the now!

It was time to focus on my heart chakra. A Hawaiian song of love played on the boom box, the breeze drifted through the window, I took in the aroma of a burning scented candle, noticed pictures on the wall honoring his teachers, and saw musical instruments in the corner.

His eyes caught mine and he spoke of playing the instruments while dancing each evening. I vowed to put even more music in my life.

With a chant to the ancestors, a hug and a kiss, an aloha (breath of life), the wisdom of how to be in the world by this island man, I was on my way ... hopefully, to have removed some blocked areas and freed my baby girl.

I realized that I was hearing wisdom more intently and choosing to change because of this exotic man in this time of relaxation. And, as I am sure my family would agree, I needed the FOUR-hour Lomi-Lomi.

P.S. It is a few years later and I am part of a group doing Sacred Healing on massage tables at Unity. It is a form of giving and receiving loving energy during a spiral opening of the chakras. This spiral was taught at the Kauai workshop of Dr. Brugh Joy where Alan offered his services. Our goal at Unity is to restore the body to its true nature. Sort of like the "baby girl" or "baby boy" state of the Lomi-Lomi!

AND A LITTLE CHILD SHALL LEAD THEM

We followed the trail into the woods near Moosehead Lake in Maine. It was our first visit and we started off to view the waterfall advertised at the end of the trail. As we walked, our eyes could only focus downward as the roots of the trees on the path challenged us to keep walking and not trip. Spring melting from the deep winter snow eroded the dirt between the tree roots.

Gradually our eyes lifted to see the dark green ferns. Low plants and ivies framed the taller grasses and shrubs. Occasionally a pine seedling provided the height that Master Gardeners seek in their landscaping. We made our way along the trail, our arms lifting limbs that had not been pruned, and our bodies deciding whether to lift legs over the fallen birch trees or do the Lindy.

Up little hills, down little hills, we came nearer the river bed, encouraging us to keep walking toward the promised waterfall. White paint on tree trunks announced the joining of a section of the

Appalachian Trail. Imagine, an eighty-year-old with his seventy-two-year-old wife hiking on the famous trail for the first time. We'd never been to Maine before and loved the solitude, surprising lack of bugs, and these majestic trees and clear river streams.

Our backs and legs began to ask if we were almost there. We saw no one on the trail. Hating to turn back without reaching our destination, we trudged ahead as the blue sky peeked through the tall trees, lighting the smaller ones. Around the next bend, we saw that the trail curved away from the stream and up ledges our legs could barely lift to carry us up. Sometimes holding onto a tree gave us a boost.

"Thank heavens," we said as we heard the bewitching sound of water rushing over rocks and down with the force of a waterfall. It had the gentle cascade of water tamed by the summer sun. We took our pictures, refreshed ourselves with a swig from our water bottle, and headed back.

Shortly we saw a fork in the trail, with the higher path and its smoother surface inviting us to try it. Before long we questioned whether we were headed in the right direction, as the footpath spread into a roadway, wide enough for logging vehicles.

The wheel ruts were deep filled, however, bespeaking of a use long ago. Small trees had fallen here and there and we worried that our legs would not get us back, especially if we had to backtrack.

She was standing in the road ahead, smiling as we approached. This little girl just appeared. Alone in her LL Bean hat, cute khaki skirt, sturdy shoes and backpack, we asked if she knew whether we were headed toward the parking lot.

"I'll show you out," she said as she turned and placed one determined foot in front of the other. I caught up with her and she said her name was Charlotte and she lived in Ireland. I was not as confident as I was before she said that, but she assured me that she had been on this trail many times. It seemed impossible for a seven-year-old from Ireland, but we followed her anyway.

An hour or so later, she spread apart two tree branches and hopped down a hidden ravine and, by golly, there was the edge of the parking lot. We plopped down on a bench and focused our tired thoughts on Charlotte.

"Where is your family? Where do you need to be?" She gave us her beguiling smile and scampered up the trail alongside the gurgling stream.

TWO ELIZABETHS, A CONTINENT AWAY

We struggled to keep the napkin on the table in the open-air South Sea island restaurant. The winds and rain buffeted the orange and black striped canvas shades on the sides of the room, ballooning them like sails on a ship.

It was the fifth day of rain for we three friends on an advertised "sun-drenched tropical island vacation." Nancy's husband had died two years before, and she had always wanted to see the world her favorite painter, Gauguin, had captured. Marge was looking for adventure, maybe an island romance with a brown-skinned hunk. I, Elizabeth, needed a respite from the care of my dad, nearing the end of his Alzheimer's journey. Dad and I shared a love of travel and he would have been happy that I spent some of the last dollars, of my fast-dwindling inheritance, on this vacation. Alzheimer's care is costly. I have to admit, though, that my husband was a bit concerned about me traveling with two unattached females.

Days before, our tiny plane had been the last to make the trip from Tahiti to Moorea before the storm hit. We settled into bed, too scared to sleep, as the wind howled, the trees outside bent nearly double, and our thatched roof began to leak. I moved my bed to a dry area while Marge and Nancy wondered aloud if we should call reception and move to another cottage.

"I'm not moving in the middle of the night," I moaned. To our amazement, the entire thatched roof sailed into the night as we watched. I couldn't get to the phone fast enough. Soon, a golf cart arrived to move our soggy selves and suitcases to dry ground.

That evening, gloom had settled over the raingear-clad travelers from France, Spain, Argentina, the United States, and even those from French Polynesia itself. I was soon startled as a huge Polynesian man put his tattooed arms around me.

"I'm Moki, you looking for a man? So sorry, me homo!"

We both giggled. I sent this six-foot-tall, two-hundred-seventy-five-pound man over to Marge. He bent over, his frizzy, bushy hair circling his big brown eyes and large-lipped face, peered into her deep blue eyes, and gently stroked her blond hair.

"Maybe you'd like to meet my wife?" he asked as a thin, *pareo*-draped man with long dreadlocks approached. The two of them put on such a show that their spirits and energy transformed the dark and gloomy mood of all the travelers. As we returned to our cottage, we rejoiced to see that the rain from the cyclone had finally stopped.

Two days later, suitcases dry and packed for our next stop, we waited in the lobby for Le Truck to take us to the big bird in the sky and, hopefully, a sunnier island. A lovely white woman with a cute ponytail manned the desk. I noticed that her shorts outfit was an American brand and she said her name was Elizabeth. We struck up a conversation and I asked about her life here in Moorea.

"I get up each morning, fix breakfast for my husband and the children, get the kids off to school, kiss my honey as he leaves for work, and then do the regular stuff; you know, washing, shopping, and food preparation for dinner." Amazingly like my life in the States.

She went on to exclaim that everyone knew each other here and looked after each other's kids, unlike Chicago where she was raised. Each year the family went to the States to visit relatives and her parents came to Moorea once a year.

"In Moorea," she continued, "I don't have to worry about kidnapping, sexual perversion, video games on the internet and TV, guns in school, or drugs. People help each other and there is no need for nursing homes for the elderly."

This Elizabeth glowed as she spoke of the philosophy of the island people. I respected the stories of the people there who take what food they need from the sea and the trees, sharing any excess with others. We spoke of churches in the States. In Moorea there is one church where all share a common value system of love and service to others.

I asked what had brought her to Moorea. She replied that she had worked for Islands in the Sun, a travel company in Chicago, and when a man from Moorea came over to do public relations, she had been impressed with him and his description of the island way of life. He courted her, and they returned to live in Moorea after their marriage.

Two Elizabeth's looked up as the driver approached the desk. I recognized the large Tahitian man who, with his dreadlocked homo wife, had entertained us that stormy night.

Moki's eyes sparkled as he grinned and said, "I see that you have met my REAL wife, Elizabeth."

GAMES

S even members of our American-Greek family went into the "Official Olympic 2004 Store." We were excited to be in Athens a month before the games were to begin. Our lunch of gyros, dolmades, and moussaka in the bustling Plaka, fortified us for shopping. We were advised to play the game of "dealing" when shopping in Greece. It goes like this: you first ask the price of the item of your choice (Qui Posso?). When the salesman states his price, you move away in a disinterested manner; as he quotes a second figure, you shake your head and frown. At this point he will tell you it's a special day and since you are their first customer, he will now offer you an unbeatable price. You turn around as if to leave the store. He pulls you back, comes up with a final lower price that will surely get him fired if the owner overhears him. The game goes on until you arrive at a price you both can live with.

The mornings were noisy with the sounds of jack-hammers and

young men arriving on juiced-up motorcycles while women shouted in the markets that the prices for the bread and fruit was, of course, way out of line. The afternoons, the hottest part of the days, were for napping and the stores were closed. It's less than a month before the Olympic opening ceremony, but Athens is asleep. Back in the states, there would be an extra crew working 24/7.

But we are in Greece and we rest and dress for our evening. The restaurants don't start serving until 9:00pm. After a delightful meal, with most of the Greeks arriving as we left, we walked back to our hotel, enjoying the cool evening. We were eager for the morning, and our first day at sea.

After breakfast rolls and coffee, we left the city for the peaceful harbor where we were to begin our five-day sail in the Sarconic Sea.

"Kalimera," (good morning) Makis, our thirty-three-year-old, bearded third-generation sailor, greeted us. We climbed aboard the ship, just large enough for the eight of us. After stowing the food and drinks we women bought at the harbor store for much of the journey, we gathered on deck to watch Makis set sail.

"Will Greece be ready for the games?" we asked. The Olympics were of great interest to our sports-minded Greek family.

"No problem," Makis answered, with a charming grin. It was impossible to tell if he was serious or whether this was the game of "optimism at all costs" so prevalent in many countries.

Then we started our own game with a simple rule. The amount spent to buy the daily fresh bread in each new port, was to be entered in the trip log. Each item for the good of all was to be written down, so we could tally up and share the burden. Food was not included in the price of the trip.

When Makis bought something for the group, he smiled, and with a typical Greek flair, smiled and said, "No problem." It did not go in the log.

Each island was different; one had hills and big trees, while another was dusty and flat. Some harbors were small and crowded, and others wide open. To our surprise, the sea also changed. One day we put on slickers, chose to continue on our way despite Makis's information that the ferries had been stopped from venturing out into the turbulent sea. He had been concerned that the two eighty-year-old men aboard would be uncomfortable. However, they smiled and said, "No problem." After all, they were Greek Americans!

Makis roared with a sailor's glee as the side of the ship touched the water and we held on for dear life. Above all, he loved the challenge of getting the most distance for the set of the sails. We were grateful as the sea calmed, and we could once again put a drink on the deck's more level table. We talked, played a few quiz games, and relaxed under the sun until we docked at our next island port. Makis joined us for Happy Hour and, full of himself for his day's successful sail, regaled us with tales of his previous sailing adventures and port escapades.

Although each island was different, we began to notice that each "Official Olympic 2004 Store" had the same merchandize, priced exactly the same. The owners growled that all Olympic shops were not allowed to discount, so we sighed and bought the Olympic souvenirs requested by family and friends at home. By not "dealing," we felt that we had lost the "purchasing game" to the smart dealers in the Olympic 2004 shop!

We returned home and, as scheduled, watched the Olympics hosted by Greece. There were "No Problems."

RASHI: SHE SHALL OVERCOME

I sat next to Rashi at a People-to-People delegation dinner in Mumbai, in 1988, when the city's name was Bombay. We Americans had read her articles in publications all over India. She dared to write of injustices to women; she risked alienation, hostility, and humiliation by sharing her personal story of being a battered wife.

Rashi was the daughter of a legendary Indian film director. During her college years, she became interested in Baahir, a young protégé of her father's, who lived in the family home. Her family strongly opposed their desire to marry. It was hard for Rashi to realize that not every man her parents liked would be approved as their son-in-law. However, he was not in her social class. Despite the fact that her father's films romanticized interclass marriages, they objected to hers. Rashi saw these protests as hypocritical, and her fight to marry him as a crusade for the elimination of class distinctions in India.

Rashi later wrote of the rape by Baahir during one college vacation, when he was especially upset with her family's rejection. She became pregnant and felt trapped. After her runaway marriage, her family disowned her, and she had to leave college. At Baahir's family home, she found his sisters, sister-in-law, and mother all utterly bound to the house, with no personal lives of their own. They all started the day at 4:00am, cleaning the house, purifying it with Ganga water, working from morning until night when the men returned at 9:00pm. The women could eat only after the men had eaten. It was a different and difficult way of life for Rashi.

Years passed and Baahir became a famous film director. He and Rashi could afford their own house now, and lived there with their three children. The year Rashi's father died, Baahir began beating Rashi and the children. Though Baahir had stopped speaking to his mother and sisters, they begged Rashi to forgive him for the beatings, because he was a famous man.

Instead, she wrote about the beatings in the newspapers. She received support from the Women's Center in Mumbai, and when I met her, she and the children were living in one part of the house while Baahir occupied the main area. Now she and the children were only subject to verbal abuse. A divorce suit had been filed three years prior, and she was hopeful for freedom soon. Since I was the only member of our delegation who had ever written for a newspaper, I was seated next to Rashi at dinner and got to know her.

Rashi told me that she was building a life for herself and her children. She worked at the Women's Center, where she helped women suffering from similar abuse. She wrote about Indian women who were also battered.

One story was about a group of Indian women who had learned from a women's group in Santa Cruz, California. They banded together, and publicly confronted a rapist at his workplace. This embarrassment was effective in India where family pride was so important. She asked me to send her stories of women and their struggles for justice in the United States. I sent a copy of Farrah Fawcett's, *The Burning Bed*, video. Her dream was to write the first

Indian film from a woman's point of view. Twenty years later, I wonder how she feels about the Indian film, *Slumdog Millionaire*, and its winning our Best Picture Academy Award.

We went to Mahatma Gandhi's residence in Mumbai, where I learned that the Rev. Martin Luther King, Jr. and his wife, Coretta, had stayed with Gandhi. They were influenced by his non-violent methods of fighting for social justice. It had moved me to hear, *We Shall Overcome,* sung many times while we were in India.

As I reflect on the progress India has made in the years since 1988, especially with improved opportunities for women in the technology area, I read that women have overcome many injustices. We have seen many changes in the past twenty years in both countries.

Rashi had courage back then to overcome her challenges, and the United States now has an African-American President. And I have overcome my reticence to publish my stories in a book.

THE HAVE'S AND THE HAVE NOT'S

She had a big city voice. We were in the Old White Lounge of the Greenbrier Resort in West Virginia listening to this trio. Ellie decided to join us on the break, and was pleased to hear our praise.

"What are you doing singing here?" we asked. Ellie answered with a kindly smile. She had come from Raleigh where she was a regular at a top club when her mother found it too difficult to care for Ellie's aging father. So, in keeping with their selfless value of placing family first, she, her husband, and their fifteen-year-old daughter sold their home and moved into the homestead in the mountains of West Virginia.

Ellie's husband had a day job, and she drove the two hours over the mountains to sing when needed at the Greenbrier. We supposed she stayed overnight but, no, she drank a cup of coffee and drove home, arriving around 3:00am, ready to take over when her husband left for his work. During those late nights, she saw many a deer in the headlights, but was fortunate never to have hit one. Ellie asked about us and we soon discovered our mutual interest in spirituality. We both were motivated to treasure family, serve others, and make the best choices we could.

Just before leaving for this trip, I had heard Allen Combs, a systems theorist, speak on "Conversations for a Better World." He proposed that our world is even more divided, into the haves and have nots, mystics and mechanics, conservatives and liberals, etc. He urged us all in this age of the internet and advanced technology, to engage in conversations with those different from us. In the process of exchange, stereotypes disappear, gaps are bridged and we find that common ground ... or common thread.

The Greenbrier is a resort primarily for Washington society. Members of the government have vacationed there since Thomas Jefferson's time. Inside the resort, the property is decorated in pinks and greens with mostly floral patterns. While the musicians stroll from place to place, the resort offers afternoon teas, fine shops, horse-drawn carriage rides, and formal dinners requiring jackets and ties. Our time there was with a son who loves history and elegance, his family and in-laws. Unfortunately, we found most of the guests' seemingly self-absorbed and not interested in conversation with new folks.

However, Ed, our waiter, was a different story. He beamed as he introduced his chunky, pony-tailed wife, who gave us a semi-toothless grin as she looked at Ed adoringly. This couple met just out of high school when Ed began his career at the Greenbrier. He tried to get into the coal mines, but there was a waiting list and when he was offered a place to stay as well as immediate work at the Greenbrier, his career as a waiter began. Ed quickly learned to say, "beautiful, a wonderful choice, excellent" no matter what we chose to order.

He told us about a white-water raft trip close by on the New River. We had a great time the next day and might have missed it but for Ed and his interest in helping his customers have a great vacation.

On the way to the river, we drove down a two-lane back road and there were the stereotypical run-down shacks with discarded refrigerators and car fenders in the front yards. Those sights and coal mines were what we expected to see in West Virginia.

Our memories, however, were of a woman named Ellie, with her values and big-city voice; Ed, who proclaimed, "It's all good"; and the contrast between the "have's" of the Greenbrier clientele and the folks who worked there.

And so we returned to Arizona, and the news and sights of Katrina, a natural tsunami that favored neither "the have's" nor "the have not's." While it initially seemed as though the decisions of the "have's" set up the opportunity for disaster, at least now they both were challenged to commit to rebuilding and share, anew, the common needs and humanity of the Have's and Have Not's.

WHAT ABOUT AMERICA/WHAT ABOUT US?

The seventy-year-old Englishman's questions were endless. "Do you ever have snow in Arizona? Why is there so much crime in America? Why can't you stop so many immigrants from entering your country?" His German wife smiled apologetically as she turned her gaze from us to the turquoise waters off the Italian coast of the Cinqueterra.

My husband and I were sailing to the first of the five villages making up this famous area of the Italian coast. Our daughter had been here a year before and had hiked the path from one village to the next. Charles, our fellow traveler, advised against walking between the last two villages, saying there were no guard rails and the path was too rocky for folks our ages and, with the wisdom of one who had been there before, advised us to take the train through the mountains.

"He finds something wrong with everything," his resigned wife interjected. In an attempt to change the subject, she directed our attention to an eleventh-century monastery atop a rugged hillside off to our left. But her husband would not be deterred.

"Don't tell me what to look at. I don't tell you!" he barked.

Turning our trapped bodies to the couple seated on the bench behind us, we were met with a sympathetic smile. Charles persisted.

"America saved our country in two world wars — we hope you don't think our opposition to the Iraqi War and George W. Bush is anti-American."

His concern about the U.S. presence in Iraq brought to mind our son's shock the day before. We had been sitting in the parlor of his Italian rental in the town of Todi, where he was staying while teaching a summer school course in art for American students. As we sipped a delightful glass of Pinot Grigio from the Villa Masetti Winery, CNN interrupted out conversation with pictures of cowering Iraqi men in the Abu Ghraib prison.

Upon hearing the announcer say, "Ivan (Chip) Fredericks is to be court-martialed and charged with high crimes for his involvement as a U.S. military man at the prison," our son's jaw dropped in amazement.

He plunked his wine glass on the coffee table saying, "Chip was my boyhood friend! We roomed together for three summers while working in Ocean City, Maryland, earning money for college. I can't believe it!"

Our daughter-in-law, an Irish woman quick to play one up-man-ship, laughed with glee.

"So, you weren't such a fine fellow after all!"

"Hey," he countered, "Chip was one of the sweetest of the bunch of us. If it's the same Chip, I'll bet he was set up. I wonder how I can help." I was proud that he valued his friendship and his belief in this boyhood friend.

We all wondered what, in America, could turn a regular young man into a forty-one-year-old capable of torturing his fellow man. We also wondered what, in England, could affect a man to become as fearful and negative as Charles.

I believe that in America, England, and other countries, we are born with the spirit of goodness. Our human experiences influence our lives and when our outer life is not attuned with our inner soul, we can make negative choices. It's not about the country, it's about the individual person. Often we miss the mark when our negative thoughts and egos obscure the Christ- or Buddha-mind we have inside.

My husband and I chose to get off the boat at the last of the five villages, and go our own way, being careful to avoid Charles. We had a delightful walk from the start of the trek to the next two villages. We made our own decision about which hikes to take and enjoyed the train ride to the last two stops.

After we got safely home to America, we did learn in a phone call from our relieved son that indeed, the Chip Fredericks of Abu Ghraib was, in fact, a different man from his friend who was still living with his family in Maryland.

So, one Chip apparently made good choices, while the other Chip made poor choices, and will be a part of the tortuous history of America and Abu Ghraib.

Every person, as well as every country, trying to do good has times when poor choices are made. We wondered what may have caused Charles to be so negative and cautious. At the same time, we realized that he had courageously married a German woman, not too many years after World War II.

Our reflections challenged us to be non-judgmental, to be responsible for our own choices, and to be forgiving of ourselves and others.

SPIRITS IN SQUAMISH TERRITORY

We gathered in the plain meeting room at the Best Western Motel in Vancouver, Canada. I was excited to have been selected as one of fifty energy healers who our California based teacher, Rosalyn L. Bruyere, had brought to the Squamish Indian tribe in British Columbia. She selects advanced students to come and minister to this tribe every other year. I had heard heart-warming stories from my energy colleagues about their unique experiences with these folks who revered Rosalyn.

The door opened and in she came. This woman, who was a remote viewer for the United States government, who traveled internationally, teaching energy healing to others, and who was regarded by scientists as one of the world's gifted healers, pulled her sweater around her well-developed fifty-year-old shoulders, and flashed her sparkling eyes as she glanced at us. She had treated brawny football players, as well as familiar movie stars, in addition to the Lakota Tribal People. She brushed her curly, long reddish hair aside as she began to speak.

"We are privileged to be here. For many it will be the first time they have let a white person touch them. I want you to all do a basic neural treatment. The majority are eighth generation fetal alcohol syndrome adults. Treat the elders first; don't mind that the grandmothers will be watching what you do, so try not to look too strange! And, they are not to be called Indians; they are First Nation People or Tribal People. Now, let's go."

We rushed toward the waiting cars ready to transport us to the Tribal gymnasium about three miles from our motel. Inside Ken, Rosalyn's partner, was waiting. This buff trainer led us in a twenty-minute Chi Gong exercise designed to warm up and energize our hands. I was amused to see some of the Tribal People get off the chairs that circled the gym and join us in the energizing exercises. Energy was noticeably rising in the room and my eagerness to begin our work as well.

We assembled around the twelve massage tables in teams of four. Rosalyn and Ken directed recipients to each table for their forty-minute energy treatment. Some would come back for each of the five days that we were there, often bringing a family member or a friend. Our days started at 10:00am and ended when the last person was seen, somewhere between 10:00 and 11:00pm.

During our meal breaks of Native people's pot-luck food, we grew in confidence as we honored each other's beaming reports of significant change stories. It was gratifying when the people we saw hugged us with appreciation after their sessions. The numbers increased each day. Young mothers brought their babies and children to us, the Tribal elders, shamans, and medicine men came as well. By the end of the week, over seven-hundred treatments were given.

On Thursday I volunteered to go out into the community with Mark, a fellow healer. We arrived at Bonnie's house and found an eighty-year-old woman, who was blind in one eye, demented, on Thorazine, and used to washing her hands repeatedly for hours upon end. Her caretaker helped her lie down on the couch as Mark and I got on our knees to place our hands on each chakra in a manner

117

Rosalyn calls a chelation. Others describe it as touching acupuncture points to remove blocks and allow energy to move through the body. All the while, Bonnie's mouth moved and we heard murmurs. When we finished, she was fast asleep and we tiptoed out, not sure that we had done any good, despite our faith in the process.

On Friday, we were asked to return to Bonnie's house. Entering, we were dumbfounded to find a coherent woman talking to a friend on the telephone. She greeted us with a smile, and reported that she felt much better and was eager for this day's treatment. As we worked, Mark and I noticed that while her mouth still moved, there were no murmurs. Her caretaker came in to gleefully remark that Bonnie had only washed her hands once since we were there yesterday. Mark and I felt such gratitude for the healing power of Spirit and Rosalyn's dedication to bringing us to this Squamish Territory.

Returning to the gym, children raced around, and Tribal members socialized while waiting their turns on the tables, and we rejoined our teams. Shawna was next. She was a beautiful, thirtyish-year-old who started sobbing as soon as she lay down. Her body began to jerk with intense emotion and we raised our hands for Rosalyn to come over. After a gentle touch to her head, Rosalyn told us she was okay and to proceed with our work as Shawna was releasing generations of pain and fear. Her sobbing subsided as the four of us, two on each side, focused on sending her love and compassion.

Shawna opened her eyes, slowly sat up, and extended her arms for hugs. "I don't mean to be insulting," she began, "but you are the first white people who have touched me with love and a desire to help. It felt fantastic and I believe I released a lot of fear and anger. When you leave, how can I continue releasing my fear and anger?"

Intuitively, I suggested that she write in her journal. Amazed, she looked at me and asked how I knew that she wrote. Silently thanking intuition, I replied, "I just did."

The tribe put on a big salmon meal for our Friday lunch, gave us all gifts, and said to please come back soon. We were grateful for this opportunity to be of service and sad that the week was almost over. I heard that my team and another had been invited to the chief's house for dinner. The eight of us had treated his only daughter. This ten-year-old had been brought by her mother, a former Hungarian princess, who wanted the best of everything for her only child.

That evening, she proudly told us of the trip they had recently taken to Toronto to introduce their daughter to the Debutante committee. We relaxed on their deck overlooking the city lights of Vancouver, looked at the chief's workshop where he made award-winning wooden carvings and highly decorated masks, and marveled at how privileged we were to be there.

Not ready to come down from the 'high' of the week, I visualized an upgrade to a first-class seat for my return to Phoenix. As I waited at the gate, I was not surprised to hear my name called and told of the upgrade. On the flight home, I read from the book I had bought describing how the Native carvers portrayed spirits in their totems and masks. I recalled how each day we had been aware of the Native spirits, as well as our own, while in the gymnasium.

As we approached Phoenix, I made a quick trip to the lavatory. Returning to my seat, I jumped up as water started soaking through my pants. My seat mate started apologizing for spilling her cup of water. Somehow, as we started our descent, I imagined spirits laughing as they manifested this way to bring me back down to earth!

THERE'S NO MACY'S HERE!

My friend, Marge, and I hopped into the jeep of the silver-haired guide hired to give us a tour of his island of Raiatea, off the coast of Tahiti in the South Pacific. Will and his wife, both Americans, had sailed the world, collected treasures from each country, and chose Raiatea as their retirement paradise. His wife had died a few years ago and now he lived here, alone, gave tours, and lectured when the big cruise ships anchored off shore. When we asked why such an attractive man had never re-married he said, "American women would have a hard time living on this island, as there is no Macy's."

This judgment of American women got to me and I was quick to tell this haughty man of my interest in the Mares of Raiatea, hoping that this more serious interest would impress on him that at least one American woman did not put shopping at the top of her sacred altar. Marge spoke of her love of Gauguin's paintings and we rolled our eyes as we headed off with Will, wondering what he would show us.

He broke the stiff silence by asking if we knew anything about the Polynesian islands and its people. I thought I'd gained some points when I mentioned that my daughter lived in Hawaii and I had learned about the culture there over the years. Seems Will had graduated from the Punahou School in Honolulu where my son-in-law now taught. I waited for the energy to change. It didn't. Marge remained silent, reluctant to play our game.

Will ambled at about fifteen miles per hour. With sarcastic delight, he remarked that he normally drove faster, but he had to have time to include additional information in his "talk" to satisfy my interest in the SPOOKS here on the island. Nary had a Tahitian passed who he did not greet, usually stopping to inquire about a family member. It was obvious that he was well known and liked here. Marge shrugged, and her eyes asked what the problem with us was?

We arrived at the site of six Mares. With reverence, rapt attention, respectful and meditative postures, we spoke of the energy we felt around the stones, remnants of the temples, placed in honor of the dead chiefs. I noticed a softening in Will and a willingness to tell us about the ancient navigational system the Tahitians developed using stars. His softness balanced the Stonehenge-like uprights comprising the old temples. We passed the altar where, long ago, the most precious sacrifice, human flesh, was offered to the gods. Since there was no known alphabet found on the island, not even on their petro glyphs, theorists believe island people communicated telepathically. I knew of the Hundredth Monkey theory, which inferred that when a changed behavior of a significant number of monkeys on one island was evidenced in monkeys on other isolated islands, it seemed unexplainable unless due to an energy communication principle.

I risked speaking of Olga Worrall, a psychic healer I had known in Baltimore, Maryland. She had gone to the Soviet Union with a delegation, including President Eisenhower's doctor, to study the Kirlian photography in use there. The energy in her healing-hands was measured before a leaf was slashed and after her hands had passed over it, restoring it to its fullness. Will knew of Olga, and this time there was no put-down comment.

We journeyed onward, stopping to visit American friends of Will's. They had retired here and Marge asked about their life, interested since she was recently widowed, loved living near the water, and was lonely. We waved farewell to our hosts and next reached the Bay of Faaraa, where Will lived. He commented that he had never had tourists in his home before, but would we ladies like a gin and tonic?

Pleased with the turn-around in his treatment of us, we wandered through his home, noticing that a portrait of him as a young man looked like Russell Crowe. We were enchanted by his collection of wood objects. He had paintings of fire-walkers on the walls, a Gauguin, which Marge admired, and we retired to his lovely deck over-looking the water, complete with sailboat. Later on our trip, Marge and I sipped Bloody Mary's at a restaurant on Bora Bora, and the owner told us that there wasn't a more knowledgeable guide in the French Polynesian islands than Will. This day, after Will returned us to our over-the-water bungalow, we thanked him for the wonderful afternoon and bid good-by, expecting to never see him again.

It didn't take me long to discover that I was missing my camera case. When I called Will, wondering if it had slipped under the seat in his jeep, he had indeed found it and suggested we meet him in town the next morning. He was to have a painting framed and offered to take us to lunch followed by a ride around the far side of the island where we could visit Mares that tourists never get to see. Having no specific plan for the day, we were overjoyed.

In town we were charmed by the French couple who owned the framing shop and both of us bought an original Tahitian piece. Will's choice of a lunch spot, as our treat, was the best restaurant in town, he said. It was Chinese! And, there were no tourists there! The Tahitian waitress giggled, seeing Will there with two ladies. He reckoned that word was spreading of his unusual behavior, where everyone's business was everyone else's.

Both the lunch and the Mares were extraordinary. We stopped on the way back to have a drink (remember it was a hot South Sea island), at another of Will's friends. These Americans, with a hilltop house overlooking the water, had retired from their life in Las Vegas. They proudly told us that their daughter had "leied" the Governor. Momentarily shocked, I then realized that she had placed a lei around his neck at some occasion.

Will's commentary slowed. The conversation turned to us. We shared travel tales. He had never been to Tibet to add to his wood art collection and he smiled when I offered to send him a piece later that year when I had a scheduled trip there. His next trip was to be to Paris for a needed back operation. Imagine my surprise when Marge suggested that he come to her lakeside home in Arizona to recuperate. She'd had two back operations and knew he'd need care. He was both silent and thoughtful. Earlier he had commented on how much better he had felt in the energy of our presence. He said that there was something different about us. He knew that I was married and settled, but Marge was not attached and he was reluctant to end his connection. We were to leave the next morning. I swallowed with delight when he suddenly asked Marge if she would come to Raiatea to care for him after his operation and, perhaps, to live.

Her reply? "Sorry, there's no Macy's here."

Part Three:
Voices of Inspiration

GRACE

I belong in this book. My story begins with the friendship between the author and a woman named Diane. Roommates at a Diadra Price led Unity retreat entitled, "Grace Awakening Essence," they focused on the spiritual, knowing that we are all energy, all part of the creative essence called God, and that it is, by grace, that we live.

Life happened, and Diane's oldest daughter tragically died of a heart malfunction. She grieved, the author grieved, the spiritual community grieved. Then, Diane went to the hospital to have a recurring heart valve problem repaired; only she didn't come back. Her spirit was strong for all and they wondered how to honor her.

The author recalled that while celebrating their Gemini birthdays, Diane looked for a Kwan Yin statue for her meditation garden. The right one could not be found that year or the next. A search started for a statue, possibly for the church's Labyrinth garden. None seemed right.

Told about a gallery in Sedona that had Kwan Yin statues, prayers for guidance were said, and the author asked Diane's spirit to let her know which, if any, were right. None of the Kwan Yin statues felt like the one. The author's eyes lifted to me, Grace.

I was on a revolving disc and, as her eyes pierced mine, I wordlessly said, "I was waiting for you to see me."

The author experienced chills. My gleaming pressed white stone and graceful lines were ethereal, angelic, reaching above. The author's heart seemed to expand and become merged with Presence.

"Could this be the right memorial for Diane?" she wondered. "Could that have been her spirit that fluffed the back of my head?"

When the saleswoman told her my name was Grace, she knew.

Diane's husband, friends, and others, contributed to bring me to the church where her husband made a perfect black marble stand for me to rest upon. The foyer was remodeled, and I have a special place allowing me to be present with my spiritual friends. I am living in a place filled with the Spirit of Grace Awakening Essence.

GRACE PRAYER
For Thee I thirst.
Into Thy hands
I commit my Spirit
(my soul, my body, my life, this problem, all unforgiven states).
Thy Will is my Will.
Thy Will be done through me.
Heal me at depth.
Reveal that which is to be revealed.
Heal that which is to be healed,
that I may glorify You, God, "I" am,
living from the Essence of Grace,
now and forevermore
into eternity's way!
It is finished!

Diadra Price
Wings of Spirit Foundation

COUNTRY WISDOM

Mrs. Ensor, the farmer's wife, gave her turkeys wine before she cut off their heads. She claimed that their lack of adrenalin before she killed them made for a tastier and moister bird. I began to notice that grocery store poultry was tougher, and I imagined the birds clutching in panic as they saw the hatchet bearing down.

Anyhow, I drove out to her farm in the countryside, near Baltimore, to buy raw milk, organic vegetables, and wine-softened turkeys when my kids were growing up in the 1960s. My new knowledge about nutrition enriched my life.

One day, I was invited to join her Sunday afternoon discussion group at the farmhouse because she thought her guest speaker would interest me. I wondered who this was as I entered the kitchen and saw simple country folk sitting around gabbing and drinking their iced tea. My curiosity and I sat in the circle and soon welcomed a four-foot ten-inch seventyish woman named Olga Worrall. Her graying hair was pulled into a bun and she was outfitted in her best Sunday housedress.

She greeted us all, thanked us for coming, and began to speak. President Dwight Eisenhower's chief physician, Dr. Dudley White, had invited her to accompany him and some research physicians from Stanford University and Walter Reed Hospital, to the Soviet Union to observe experiments using Kirlian photography. Whoa! She had my attention.

Olga told us that such photography let people see energy and then measure its effects. She had been invited because of her sensitive hands. Olga and her late husband, Ambrose, were renowned energy healers, having the New Life Clinic in downtown Baltimore. Her hands had been inside a Faraday Box at Stanford University and her energy was the highest the scientists ever measured; thus, her invitation to the Soviet Union.

Olga showed us photos of an experiment. First, they photographed a leaf, slashed it with a knife, and then took a new picture. Next, Olga placed her hands over the leaf. The last photo showed the leaf whole again!

Olga and Ambrose were known in the healing community for placing their hands on people at their clinic in Baltimore for years, where many healings had occurred.

I was blown away that Sunday afternoon in the knotty pine room at the farmhouse. I had seen a white light over the leaf when Olga's hands were above it. I was a counselor in the profession of helping people, but this was healing! What did these country folk know about energy that I hadn't heard of in my professional studies? I had changed my choice of foods through knowing Mrs. Ensor. That afternoon I embarked on another significant life change.

A few years later, I returned from leading a communications work-shop in Vermont with Dr. Sid Wolf. Sid was a psychologist who had written his doctoral dissertation on what led to changes in people. Neither their educational degrees, nor the type of therapy practiced, led to significant change. His research determined that it was the degree to which therapists, or people in general, had developed ten core qualities within which facilitated change.

That morning he had offered me some raw bran to add to my cereal. Always interested in improving my health, I accepted. On the flight home to Baltimore, I experienced alarming stomach pain. Sid leaned over and asked if I wanted him to rid me of the pain. Did I ever!

As he held my hand and focused, I felt the pain move from my stomach, up my chest, and down my arm. As it left my hand, he broke contact and shook his hand before repeating the process ... until the pain was gone.

"What did you do?" I asked in amazement.

With a twinkle in his eye, he said that when it was time for me to know, I would learn. Like the day with Olga, I realized I had a lot to learn about energy.

Retirement has given me the time to do some of the things I put aside when I was raising kids and working long hours. I began studying energy and its part in healing. A teacher, Rosalyn L. Bruyere, does what Olga and Sid showed me, and even more. I meet with a group of her students once a week to explore new galaxies of energy information and offer hands-on healing to others. Every Wednesday evening, energy workers offer loving energy at our local Unity Church as part of our healing/prayer service. I can feel the dense presence of energy now, my hands are warm and tingling with electricity. I have studied how to increase energy, and am with others who can see it.

Last week a member of our group brought a book, written years before, that she found fascinating. The author was a woman named Olga Worrall.

GIFT OF THE REAL ESTATE RAPIST

A flyer circulated to realty offices in Phoenix, Arizona, with a police sketch of the man dubbed, "the Real Estate Rapist." It was one more thing stuffed into her broker's desk drawer. Linda was referred to me for a pre-trial evaluation shortly after I started my counseling practice in Phoenix. Never liking prospective court cases, I agreed, as, after all, it was a job. After it turned out to be so much more for both of us, I emailed my story to Linda the other day to ask her permission to use it. This is what she wrote back:

"Reading Elizabeth's story tonight brought back so many memories that have long been stored in a special place. This place is not of anger or pain, anymore; it is one of gratitude for the opportunity to piece together my life. Now don't misunderstand me, rape is not a route you want to take to get to know yourself! But, it was my ride, and what a ride it was!

"As a child, I always had an ability of knowing when things were going to happen to people, and if I was liked by my childhood friends. Since I had no one to validate, or explain, those bizarre experiences, I quickly put them away as best as I could. Needless to say, I sure had a lot of questions but, being a good Southern girl, I knew to not go there with the family.

"My life went on to a marriage, two children, divorce, and a son with drug issues. It appeared to be a life of drama and anguish. Again, the visions and inner-knowing multiplied, but I was not having any thing to do with them. It was a time for "getting through" my perceived hell. Yet, all the while the help was coming in and, as usual, I had deaf ears to it.

"Time moved on, and years later I had a new husband and a cross-country move to the Southwest. Having spent most of my career traveling for corporate America, I decided to start this marriage off with a nine-to-five career and couldn't believe my luck when I found a job selling condos for a local real estate community. My second day produced my first sold unit, and I was excited to get to the office the next morning, sure I would meet this day with equal success.

"The car pulled up, and the feelings came over me with the strong energy shooting up from my feet to my head. These old feelings of danger just couldn't be true! I quickly put them aside and met the young man with a sale on my mind. He left shortly and promised to bring his wife back to see the models later in the day. I remember scolding myself for even paying attention to the danger I felt.

"He was back in an hour, asking to see some of the designs for the units. Again, the feelings, but it was too late. The knife was at my throat, and the rest was the beginning of the nightmare that followed me through a hell for years to come.

"One month later, the new husband was gone and I was alone in a new city with family and friends three-thousand miles away, facing a court case to put a rapist away, and afraid to walk into the closet for clothes. I needed help.

"The feelings were back with a new twist, a voice I had heard before but a lot clearer than before. The words were forceful in saying, 'step out of the house, the correct help will come.'

"Days passed as I would sit in a stupor, afraid, and sure I was not hearing the childhood voices, just my own crazy voice.

"I really don't remember how I found Elizabeth Kaites, but I knew the message was correct and I had found a lifeline in more ways than one. Not only did she get me through the trial and his sentencing, and counseling for my PTSD, but she reunited me with trust in others.

"After our counseling was no longer necessary, and a few years passed, we met again and she became a friend for this lifetime, and probably many more. It is comforting to know that our lives are intertwined, and the teaching of my self-respect has been facilitated by this beautiful spirit.

"Time has gone on, and I have learned forgiveness, joy, hope, and empowerment, knowing that the beings that have been with me are here to stay. They have shown me how to believe I have a gift to share. Nowadays, I am a counselor, of sorts, as a Feng Shui Master and I give intuitive readings, search for dead people for the Phoenix police, as well as help find missing live souls.

"The move to Phoenix would prove to be a blessing, as I have been given an opportunity to get back in touch with who I was created to be, and to be of service to others."

Over the years since, I have kept up with Linda. First, I read that she was giving a lecture on Feng Shui at the nearby Borders bookstore. My husband and I went, came home with a green and red mirror to place near our front door for luck, and a promise to see each other again soon.

More years passed before Linda called to tell me that her stiff limbs and frog-like face were from Lupus. It didn't seem fair that she should have to deal with this, too; but, as they say, life isn't fair. However, I believe that what's important is how we deal with life's challenges.

When I retired and arranged to move to Prescott, I asked if she'd meet me for lunch to look over my furniture placement. Her cane hung over the chair as she moved the small pieces of paper I had measured out around the paper rooms. While she did her Feng Shui magic, she told of her son's continuing drug problems and the new, unsettling phone calls from the jail where her attacker was incarcerated. I worried about this stress in her life.

My last face-to-face was when she had her old face back and no cane. She wore a pretty coral pants suit, bought with money from a vision leading police to a remote spot in the Arizona desert where a missing man's body was found. I was pleased that her psychic powers were being put to good use. She spoke of knowing Allison DuBois, the "real" *Medium* of television fame.

As for Linda, she was planning to return to her childhood home of Atlanta, Georgia, where her daughter and grandson lived. I was happy for her to be going far away from the soon-to-be-released rapist and into the arms of loving family.

I thought she belonged in my collection of memorable people and wrote a story and mailed it to her. She mailed me the reply. However, neither her psychic abilities, nor my lack of computer skills, could resurrect the original story. So, believing in things happening for a reason, I decided to let you read about the Real Estate Rapist and the gift Linda felt it gave her, from her own point of view.

LEARNING HOW TO BE IN THE WORLD

We nine healers had come together in Happy Jack, Arizona, to deepen our ability to *Be* in the world. "It was to be like one grown-up pajama party for therapists," I told my puzzled husband, since we gals had not spent time away from our therapy practices to be with each other for months.

The facilitator, who stood in front of us that first morning on the outdoor deck in the dense woods, had flowing white hair and green eyes. She looked centered and glad to be with us. She commented that it took the nine of us awhile "to come to sitting."

Her eyes glimmered with humor, and her serene smile both welcomed and challenged us. We had contracted to spend the weekend at a colleague's mountain retreat with this respected "therapist's therapist." My eyes left the mountain pines out the window to the lit candles on the fireplace hearth and back to her.

She began by asking us, gently, to "come to standing." Just as I got balanced on my feet, we were asked to, "come to sitting."

What was this about???

We spent that weekend being led through exercises designed to focus us on the present and on our feelings, not *thinking* or *doing*. She asked us to be aware of how we felt when we rose to stand, and instructed us to *be more present* by staying with these feelings.

Those of us who thought we knew how to live more fully in the *now*, believed that we just had to keep our thoughts on the here and now, less on the past and future, and that was the secret.

"Not so," she claimed. "If we stand and are thinking of something else, we are in the past or future, not all present."

Our next challenging question, "How do you define healing?" was one that surely one of the nine of us healers present could manage. Some of the words tossed around were *balance, wholeness, flow, acceptance, energy, effortlessness,* and *restoration.*

"Healing is to tap into Infinity," she offered and, "the gateway to Infinity is the Now. Life Eternal flows effortlessly through us; we have within all we need, and Infinity has been with us from the beginning."

I thought about how effort did not produce results in my life as much as the times when I allowed what was within to emerge. I also thought about how our pastor explained that when we pray, God always says yes, but the trick is to bring ourselves into congruence with the Eternal Spirit and Divine Law.

In *The Book of Mary Magdalene,* the author writes about the inner place where creative imagination resides, and we are in the flow. There were other's who had written or spoken of Bliss, Oneness, or experiences that seemed to express what she was talking to us about. I was beginning to get on her wave length.

Okay, I thought, so I am to be aware, to accept what is, and then take action. I realized that most of the time I moved from awareness to action. Taking a moment to center puts me into a higher consciousness from which to take action. When I accept and have only positive feelings instead of resistance, fear, or other negative emotions, my actions are more loving and positive and, therefore, more effective.

This thought was consistent with my engineer husband's oft quoted phrase, "I don't believe in luck. It's when preparation and opportunity come together."

He also quotes Dr. David Hawkins, who writes about raising consciousness from the lower energy levels (two-hundred or below) toward a five-hundred level, where Love resides. Jesus and Buddha functioned at this level. Research stated in his book, *Healing and Recovery*, supports this doctor's theories. I was sure ready for a mid-morning break to integrate my thoughts and clear my head.

Iced tea and homemade sandwiches tasted good and brought me down to earth! The afternoon commenced with a discussion of wings.

"One is the Universal," she said, "and the other, the Individual Soul." She drew what looked like a butterfly, with the center the dwelling place of God. I thought I got it. When our center is of God, and half of us is filled with what is universally true, and the other half is our individual soul, we can fly. We're not stuck in our blockages and, therefore, are able to rise in consciousness. Also, with love allowing us to overpower the subconscious, we rise closer to peace and joy.

Another teacher once said, "Whenever two or more are gathered together, there will I be also." We discussed our realization that change must go through our cores.

The first day was over! We walked through the woods, picked wildflowers, listened to the birds, kept an eye out for the local deer, and returned refreshed and energized. After a wonderful dinner of lasagna and salad, we played, and, as the saying goes, "What happens in Vegas, stays in Vegas."

The next morning began with meditation, stretching exercises, and then some tea and rolls. We gathered on the deck, ready for the day's challenges. She began, "When you hear an idea or are asked to do something that you don't agree with — and don't speak your truth — resentment builds, and no change can take place in you nor in the other. Also, if you agree to gain approval, in order to not make a scene, it becomes an act of violence on yourselves."

Memories flooded my mind of times when I had kept my 'different' opinions to myself, or kept silent during a dinner table conversation when my husband had said, "Elizabeth believes" or "Elizabeth does" ...

when I lacked the courage to say, "Not exactly." Or even when visiting my grown children I had kept quiet about a difference in parenting that could have resulted in our grandchildren's benefit.

So many times I have kept my opinion to myself when I thought it wouldn't be either prudent or popular to express it. How many times have I cheated others or, more importantly, myself, of stretching understanding. How many times have I kept quiet when my husband raised his voice to express an opinion and, because I was reluctant to cause unpleasantness, I lost self respect and often the respect of others? I silently made a vow to be more myself in my world.

"To truly transform, we must be comfortable with the Angel of Impermanence," she next offered.

I do *know* that nothing lasts forever. When and where am I holding on to the notion that I am always the same? Am I willing to be vulnerable to myself in order to change my story? Can I get out of my future wishes and my ego's desires? Can I live more in the center where my soul taps into the Great Spirit or God?

I looked off into the mountain air and recalled when a wise friend told me that my life was too small for the soul I have. I was flattered that he thought I had a large soul, but thoughtful as to how I was to open up my life to a larger and wider one. In some ways, the road was one of surrendering personal desires and control, and letting what happened stretch me beyond my imagining.

We were challenged to think of ourselves as having built walls around us at vulnerable points to protect our feelings. Could we let the walls down and live more in our center with the spark of Divine that also lives there? Could we trust? Could we fly like a butterfly?

As time has gone on since that day in Happy Jack, I have found that living a more conscious life, practicing many of the therapist's ways of being in this world, has enabled me to come to *being*. A friend has commented that I am a lot more real and interesting since I have begun to share more of my opinions. I've noticed that we get invited out more since I "take others on" when appropriate. I am no longer seen as an extension of my husband and his ideas. Why, I can even admit to not always voting the way he does in national elections!

With twinkling eyes, others have indicated that this last election split more families than mine. Perhaps when we each speak our truth, with our loved ones and in our world, creativity and more balanced solutions can emerge to benefit us all. It takes a lot of living to learn how to *be* in the world!

DREAMS

P at began, "I had this dream last night with you, and my friend, John, from Pennsylvania, sitting at a table in a restaurant. You have to join John, my husband and me, for dinner Saturday night when he arrives from out of town."

I chose not to date since my marriage ended six months before, so I was surprised by this dream and its invitation.

"I'm sorry, but I promised my daughter a visit this weekend with her friend who lives in the Pocono's. We'll be back in Baltimore Sunday afternoon. If you haven't found a date for him for Saturday and you want to go out Sunday for dinner, call."

Pat and I had worked as Directors of Christian Education at local churches, years before, and now were both working at Towson High School.

Sunday, chicken was in the oven, our wet bathing suits in the laundry, and we were unpacking gear from the weekend, when the phone rang.

"We'll be out in a half hour, and wear a long dress. John is so anxious to meet you."

I had completely forgotten this possibility and said that I needed forty-five minutes. Five minutes later, my ex-husband arrived with our son. They had returned from a six-week camping trip out West.

"Could I run a couple of loads through the washer before leaving?" he asked.

"Could you take the chicken out of the oven and feed the children?" I asked. Deal.

There was an immediate connection between John and me that evening. Perhaps it was the two-day buildup about me that my friend, Pat, gave to John. She had met this divorced man at a human relations workshop a couple of years before. He visited Pat and her husband in Baltimore whenever he had business in Washington.

Each summer John's son would come east to spend time with his dad, and when summer ended, and the inevitable teary plane departure came, John eased his sad loneliness by getting out of town. As was his custom, he asked Pat and her husband to line up a date for the evening.

After my separation, I had prayed that God would choose a man for me to share my life. John had prayed that he not live life alone, and that he would find a spiritual partner.

We kept up a long-distance courtship, and were talking about how to combine our families and lives, when a friend from church called and asked me to lunch. She had dreamed of a sailing trip in the Bahamas and her husband had encouraged her to arrange it for after Christmas. The sailboat had room for three couples and she had asked Mary and me for lunch to consider the trip. Mary had also met John at the church workshop. The offer was tempting for us, as our marriage was planned for Christmas. We agreed that we would meet the other two couples for a sailing trip after a weeks honeymoon. These two dreams started John and me on a wonderful journey together.

We were drawn to Dr. Brugh Joy's workshops years into our marriage and experienced his analyzing people's dreams. He believes this is how our inner voice, one with that of God, is heard. I also believe that when we dream, our inner wisdom can more freely create possibilities. Some wonder if in a timeless world, perhaps we see glimpses of what we refer to as the future.

Just yesterday, a woman who had experienced Sacred Healing Meditation at our Unity Church told me that she had a dream showing the entire lower floor of the church filled with healing tables. We've already gone from two tables to eleven. I'm always ready to hear and believe a dream!

THE DEFAULT SEX THERAPIST

I had no real training for this. Just because I was a female counselor in small Johnstown, Pennsylvania, with its five male psychiatrists, was no reason to send me all the folks with sexual problems. Even the one male OB-GYN in town soon started referring his women patients who whispered about being less than satisfied by their lovers when they came for their yearly exams.

Should I admit to not being specially trained in sex therapy? I was new in town, just building up my practice, willing and ready to give it a go. After all, wasn't I a happily married mother of four?

So, I bought all the books I could find on sex therapy: tantric; Kinsey's; Masters and Johnson; David Schnarch's, *Passionate Marriage*; and even subscribed to a newsletter entitled, *Sex Over Forty*. As I was absorbing these tomes I discovered that most of the couples had communication problems, not sex problems. Well, shoot, I was a nationally traveled workshop leader in communication skills ... no problem.

It was my day off when my husband called to surprise me by saying that he was on his way home for lunch. I gleefully scurried into the guest room, closed the blinds, put our satin sheets on the bed, lit a candle, put on my most inviting teddy, and opened the door to a very startled man.

"Do you have to rush back to the office?" I purred.

When he regained his breath, he exclaimed, "You got your *Sex Over Forty* newsletter in the mail today, I bet!" Of course, I denied the truth.

Word quickly spread that this sex-therapist had marvelous suggestions for pepping up aging folk's sex lives. My secretary even started asking for copies of the newsletters she was printing for clients. Each new issue was more informative than the next. Why, we were dealing with E.D. before the television commercials made it a commonly known dysfunction.

There was the man who liked to sneak into his wife's closet and dress up in her clothes, complete with Estee Lauder, who sheepishly arrived with his indignant wife. She was not amused by his behavior. I had my work cut out for me. Still, I discovered the situation to be more a matter of communication and negotiation than a sexual issue.

Another client was puzzled as to why he "got off" on women's pantyhose. When I inquired about early memories and heard that at age five he had hid on the upper staircase while his parents made out on the downstairs couch, I had a clue. Hearing that he saw his mom's leg go up in the air, first with panty hose on and then saw his dad slowly take them off, I knew I had uncovered the source of the fetish.

I learned about Dom's and Sub missives from my clients as I listened with the calmness of an experienced, know-it-all sex therapist. Somehow I managed to help them or refer them out. Pittsburgh was an hour and a half up the road and there were lots of *real* sex therapists in that big city.

My experience taught me that couples who had fantastic sex lives before or during counseling could divorce, that couples who had so-so sex lives could stay together happily, that any unusual fetishes or early life challenges could be overcome or used to advantage, and that everyone could use a little spice now and then. Basically, the more important qualities of a happy relationship were communication, commitment, caring, and having a non-judgmental attitude. At least, that's today's wisdom from the mouth of this, by default, sex therapist.

I AM A MIRACLE

He went over to her at the beginning of the last day of our workshop in Body Psychology. His suave movement, well-groomed hair and attire, was in sharp contrast to her frumpy, disheveled hair, pinned carelessly atop her head. Without a word, he invited her to the table set up in the circle of the eighteen participants, college graduate students in art therapy.

"Oh, no," she stammered, in her broken Russian accent, "I've never done anything like this before."

"Don't you think it's time for you?" came the smiling voice of the leader, as he gently placed an arm on her shoulder.

She slowly raised her quivering body onto the edge of the table. Her head was bowed.

His eyes were full of compassion and encouragement as he asked, "What is going on with you?"

The tears started to flow immediately as this middle-aged woman shook her head back and forth, keeping her head down. He ever so smoothly and gently helped her lie down on the table and waited.

"I am so scared," she began.

"Yes," he nodded, and repeated, "You're so scared." Her story spilled out so fast we could hardly grasp the details.

"My father was a big man, tough, most always drunk. He beat my brothers and me with a wooden log. I still have headaches a lot of the time.

Her sobs muted our tears. Through her gasps she told of leaving home when pregnant with the first of three children, only to repeat the fear as her husband came home drunk to beat her and the children.

She managed to leave him, and run away to America. Here she met and married a man with two children she raised with her own.

"He, too, was so mean," she said of this husband. And when the children left home, she flew this coop. She went to school, graduated college, and came west to start anew.

"How is this for you, so far from your children?" the therapist asked.

The tears flowed again as she chokingly said that her children were married and didn't need her anymore, so she left to get out of their lives.

"You also did it for you," he lovingly suggested.

"But I didn't completely get away as I feel my father's presence even here!" she sobbed.

"Is he alive?"

"No, he died five years ago."

"He's here," the leader suggested, "tell him ..."

But her shoulders shook with fear. "Oh, no, not here," she cried.

"Tell him to go away, that you're glad he can't hurt you anymore and that this is your time to be free."

"I'm glad you're not here," she said, tentatively then louder, "I'm glad you're not here!

"God helped me get away from him and come to this wonderful country. There are nice people here and good things. But, are you sure God will not be angry at me for not wanting my father around me?"

146

The leader shook his head as he assured her that he believed God was within and was of love, and would not want her hurt anymore.

"It is a miracle that I survived, "she whispered.

"It is a miracle that you had the strength to leave Russia and come to America. God helped, but your feet carried you here," he said with firmness as he stroked her arm, ever so gently. She only looked in his eyes. Those of us sitting in the circle were silently sending her love and energy to believe in herself.

She began again, "I am scared to drive in big cities. I have an interview next week, and I am afraid I won't be understood with my accent."

"You and I are talking just fine," he stated with a supportive smile.

"Yes, but you are helping me so much, you are a miracle."

"No, you are the miracle," he said with love, and we all shook our heads in agreement.

"Now, say, 'I am a miracle.'"

No words from her. She swung her body up into a sitting position, again with her head low. "I am horrible; no make-up and an old woman," she said.

"You are a miracle. Look around at the faces in the circle. What do you see?"

"They are smiling and look so happy."

"Yes, they see a miracle."

One of the women leaned forward in her chair and said, "Don't you ever put yourself down again."

"Oh," she exclaimed as she straightened up, "I don't have a headache anymore."

"And," offered the therapist, "I am a Miracle!"

This rosy cheeked woman straightened her skirt, held her head high as she walked around the room looking each of us in the eyes saying, "I am a Miracle!"

BLINKY

This Army man, newly returned from Iraq, sat next to me on my Northwest flight from snowy Baltimore, Maryland, headed for sunny Phoenix, Arizona. We both looked nervous as the arm of a de-icing machine outside sprayed yucky looking liquid over the icy wings of our plane.

"I felt safer in a plane in Iraq," Ken stated. "At least I had my parachute on then."

Not reassuring, I thought. Eager to keep my mind off the anti-freeze keeping us from seeing outside, I asked him about his most memorable mission in the Special Forces. He gave me an amused smile, pulled up the shirt sleeve revealing a tattooed arm, and said that his mother, a woman younger than I, didn't want to hear about his adventures, not even where he was as he moved around the world.

I replied that I was a writer and, not having to worry about him, I wanted to hear.

"Well, it was a night flight over the border of Iraq and Afghanistan," he began. They were to parachute over Iraq and walk the four miles into Afghanistan. As the first team member jumped, a gust of wind took him off course and it looked to Ken, the team leader, that he was headed for Afghanistan. The stripes on the jumper's jacket were visible with Ken's night vision glasses, and he saw that his buddy was being blown off course.

The light went off in the plane signaling Ken and the others to jump. They looked like twinkling stars in the night sky with their special glowing stripes. Fumbling with his rip chord and his radio, Ken instructed the errant jumper to hide and stay quiet. The team would start their walk and, hopefully, meet up with him.

Ken and I talked of the importance of teamwork in all areas of life. In the Army Special Forces, it was necessary for survival. He told me that one of the most important trainings for the people living in the outer villages of these two countries was to teach them to work together. If one family was attacked, the neighbors could assist and surround the attacker and provide a chance for survival.

I shared the message of the play, *Well*, that I had seen the day before. The mother in the play had worked to racially integrate the neighborhood as her daughter was growing up. In adulthood, as the daughter returned, she only wanted to acknowledge the "good" people in the neighborhood, while the mother spoke of the strength when all are integrated, saying there is no perfect good or bad and we need the strengths of all.

This wisdom could be applied to Ken's team, to relationships, integrated neighborhoods, and to our world.

My thoughts went to the power of light, as the one team member was able to be reunited with his team in Afghanistan because of light. My college boyfriend had made me a reminder of his love by painting a baking soda box shiny brown and installing a little blinking light in the top. I named it "Blinky" and it sat on my desk in my dorm as a reminder that I wasn't alone in my new world.

As a professional therapist, I later had a "Chi Lite" in my office for clients to put on areas of their body needing extra love and energy.

Years later when I was dealing with a breast tumor, Dr. Wilson suggested that we build a sauna with three infrared lights that emitted healing light focused on my breast. Was it that light, prayers, or all of the above that allowed the tumor to disappear?

Often, I hear people telling others who ask for healing or safe travel that they will "be held in the light." I believe this means in the presence of God, our creator. My favorite Biblical verse has been, "Let your light so shine that they may see your good works and glorify your Father which is in heaven."

The engines roared, we started racing down the runway and lifted off into the sky, stronger for the de-icing, and more at ease because of our conversation. Ken's wink reminded me of Blinky, and we each returned to our own worlds.

MARIA ELENA

This woman's eyes bore into my soul. "She knows," I thought to myself. She knows that part of me waits until its safe to come out. She knows that I build walls around expressing extreme emotions, and that I have spent most of my life going to school, achieving, being logical, successful – even in my profession, one that requires graduate degrees and continuing education.

But she knows it's difficult for me to allow myself to emote.

I knew this when I was twelve years old, sitting under a tree at church camp, praying to God that He would gift me with the ability to feel deeply, like Nettie Dean, one of our counselors. Nettie just plain glowed! She felt through her body, deep into the earth. She prayed a lot and shook when she called upon the Lord; so I tried to pray harder.

How I yearned to express passion in my passionless home and life. Mother and Dad never let my brother and me be silly or angry, or anything they deemed excessive. But when I looked at Nettie Dean, I sensed I was missing out on something.

"I'm here to help women, like you, recovering your feminine soul, your connection to Mother Earth," said Maria Elena, an earthy Mexican woman who led workshop-gatherings in her home.

She gently asked me to uncross my legs, suggesting that I block energy coming from the earth into my body this way. Since I still didn't have that glowing, I believed that I was doing something to block it. Uncrossing my legs was a small change I could easily make and, wow, it might let enough energy into my body to let me glow. But I still didn't glow.

Women like me. Well, we did have those degrees in common. All of us were some sort of professional. Nettie Dean hadn't been an academic and neither was this Maria Elena. They also didn't seem to be "proper ladies" like my mother, who sat with legs crossed.

Now that I think of it, I read an article once that suggested that if you crossed your arms or legs, it was a sign you were being defensive. Defensive about what? I certainly wanted whatever needed to happen that would allow me to feel deeply.

Now, she said, to lie on the floor and put a black mask over our eyes.

The music was soooo loud. The floor moved when the drums played, and I thought I could hear someone crying. I wanted the music to stop. I like music, but not so loud. Thank God it finally ended. Maria Elena was smiling as we took off our eye shades.

"What did you feel?"

I said that the music was too loud. One of the women was transported back to a time in her childhood that was painful, and she cried. Maria Elena seemed pleased with that sharing. In groups like this, no one talks, they "share."

I just knew the floor moved and the music was too loud — I didn't "feel" anything. But I sat with my legs uncrossed, and hoped.

I went back to Maria Elena because I knew she knew. This time I was alone. It cost a lot of money, but it would be worth it if I could learn to express deep feelings and glow like Nettie Dean. We didn't talk long before Maria Elena took me into a room with a table prominently in the center. I had seen tables like this in massage therapist's offices. I was to take off my outer clothes, leave on my underwear, and lie under the sheet.

When she came back into the room, I could smell something sweet burning. She rubbed some lotion into her hands before she touched me. This time the music was soft. I guessed you could learn to feel whether the music is loud or soft. I closed my eyes.

With soft music, you don't need eye shades. I felt soooo relaxed. I didn't need to think about anything. I rather enjoyed the touching. When I felt the air move above me, I peeked. Maria Elena was, passing a peacock feather over me and smiling.

Feeling seemed to be a matter of unblocking the walls I had built. I recalled a time when my father asked why I didn't look at him the same way I looked at my 16-year-old boyfriend. I clutched inside. I remembered deciding to protect my feeling self by being a very intelligent daughter and less affectionate.

Could I have built a wall with others, as well, and kept myself from a lot of my feelings? Perhaps God had gifted me with feeling all along.

Then it came to me that I had always *felt* deeply, I just wasn't a deeply expressive person, and what I had really been seeking was the joy that I and Spirit were one. That's what made Nettie Dean glow.

I sensed that I had begun to glow with new awareness as I left Maria Elena's.

THE CHOICE

Don was busy finalizing his Christmas sermon when the phone rang and interrupted his concentration. There was so much to do this Christmas Eve day: the evening services to get ready, e-mails to tend to, and chairs to set up in the extra room for overflow worshipers. Since Prescott was a small town between Phoenix and Route 40, there were lots of travelers.

"Yes, he answered, how may I help you?"

The man's voice on the other end sounded young and, oh, so tired. Don heard a baby's cry in the background.

"Could you spare money for gas and maybe for a room for the night? My wife and baby slept in the car last night. We don't have money for gas to help us on our way."

Don sighed. How was he to decide whether this was a real cry for help or a wino's con? He asked his secretary how much money the church had in its fund to help those in need. The calls were usually for food, however.

Something in Don, perhaps because it was Christmas Eve, called him to respond, "Where is your car ... I'll meet you with some money."

On the way to the center of town and the post office where they were to meet, Don was startled to hear on his car radio the story of Mary and Joseph, the night Jesus was born.

He couldn't help but wonder about this young couple and their babe that he was to meet. His sermon preparation focused upon how we are challenged each day to respond as Jesus would.

Didn't the Bible say "as much as we did it unto the least of these, we were doing it unto Him?"

He had remembered hearing of a friend's visit with Mother Teresa, years before, and having her say to the group of American's, "Go back to your country, and whenever you help the poor and needy there, you are serving God, just as I am here in India."

Was this one of those times? Could this be a modern-day challenge to faith and would his response be more loving than the Innkeepers? Or, was he being foolish with the congregation's offerings. After all, they trusted his judgment.

Arriving at the post office, Don saw only one car parked outside, an old Chevy with lots of body rust. Across the street, the town square glowed with Christmas lights and the streets reverberated with recorded carols and ringing bells.

Don slowly got out of his car. The young father lowered his window and reached out his dirty hand. As Don placed the clean white envelope into his outstretched hand, he glimpsed into the window. He hoped that whatever he saw would answer his questions. The woman was rocking her baby and barely looked up. The young man acknowledged the gift and started rolling up the window.

Don sighed, no more sure of the rightness of his action than before. He opened his car door, turned the heater on and slowly started driving back to the church. His mind kept replaying the Christmas story of yore and the coincidence of a young family, traveling this Christmas Eve day, with no place to lay their heads.

If any of us ever knew for sure that we were helping the parents of

155

Jesus, or a couple who have the Divine Spark within, wouldn't that be an easy decision? Doesn't our faith teach that we each are responsible for our choices in life?

He recalled an old Buddhist parable in which the Buddha dressed as a beggar and revealed himself only to the one compassionate man who helped him. Anyhow, Don smiled and thought to himself, "Don't we believe that the Divine lives in us all?"

Don arrived at the church parking lot, got out of the car and opened the door to his office.

"Well?" his secretary asked, with her eyebrows raised.

"I don't know about them," Don answered with a smile. "I just know about me, and I know that I responded with love this Christmas Eve."

THE MULTIPLE

She lay on my office massage table in a fetal position. Her sobs were those of a three-year-old.

"Susie wants a pair of Mary Jane's," she whined. "You promised me."

I both soothed and reassured Susie that her mother, the host personality in this multiple, would look for the special shoes, and then challenged her to organize the younger kids (voices in this adult's chaotic head), so her mother could talk to me.

My sixty-one-year-old client straightened her skirt, got off the table, and sat down on the leather chair. She smoothed her page boy chestnut brown hair, and gave me a grown-up smile.

"This energy work is helpful," Judy exclaimed. "The children feel loved and settle down earlier each day."

I wondered aloud how Judy, the host personality, was coming along with her writing.

"Susie and her desire for shoes has kept me from working today."
Judy took out some artwork done earlier in the week that was for her
book. I saw vivid colors and indistinct images, somehow fitting for a
"How To" book dealing with early childhood trauma.

Judy was the first-born of two bright, but disturbed, parents. For as
long as she could remember, her mother had "given" her to her father,
sexually. And father indulged. So did grandfather and several uncles.
Typical of such abused children, she married at the first opportunity to
get away from the family.

Her immature marriage didn't last long, but long enough for her to
get a college degree and the means to support herself. When life's
stresses increased, the children's voices in her head took up more and
more time to settle in the mornings, so no job lasted too long.

Dates, when Judy wanted to go dancing or venture out to a nice
dinner, were short lived. To tell the new suitor about herself or not
was always the question. And, besides, how long can you keep
refusing sex?

Then there was the matter of pride. Dad was tired of bailing her out,
financially, and the brothers couldn't understand why she didn't have
a decent job, especially since she now had earned a Master's degree.

Judy wanted to help others deal with their trauma by writing her
book and, perhaps, starting a home for abused adults; but Susie and
the others took so much of her energy.

The one time she started to tell her brothers of her early sexual abuse
they quickly shut her down in disbelief and outrage.

I met Judy when she came to a free demonstration of energy work.
She said it really helped calm her and wanted to come regularly. She
seemed so mature and smart, that when she pleaded poverty and
asked to trade for the sessions, I agreed, believing our work would be
short lived.

Then I met Susie, an adult male named Charles, and the others in
her head. My work turned out to be long enough for her to direct lots
of "stuff," her mother had unloaded upon her, in my direction.

Our work began with identifying all the players; then organizing
them into teams, according to age and ability. The children were soon

organized each morning and Judy began to have a life. Our energy work on the table released a lot of past trauma. She began writing and drawing. It took less and less time to organize the family.

Judy needed support whenever she had a "command performance" with the aging parents. We structured these visits to be minimally stressful. She chose to keep in reasonable touch, and in their good graces, since there was a sizable inheritance possible that would help her accomplish getting her book published and setting up a service for traumatized women. She felt that this would give meaning to her fractured life.

One of the men personalities inside her head kept taunting her and questioning any self-worth. Judy had a spiritual core which strengthened her during these times. We practiced affirmations to repeat so she could transform that male's inner statements.

As she became healthier, she decided to rename herself to symbolize her whole and healthy God-created self. From then on, I made appointments with Lauren. Soon after, I was invited to a dream presentation that she was scheduled to give in town. I went, and it was quite good. She began exploring the possibility of teaching.

At this stage, I never asked about the children, nor did I hear from them. Lauren was doing well in town attending dances, dating, and, from time to time, I'd see her at a lecture. Our sessions stopped.

A year later, I got a call from her inviting me to a presentation she was giving on dreams at the college where I was an advisor. I was doing a workshop in a nearby room at the same time.

Later, I heard comments from students saying this lady "really knew what she was talking about" and had given a wonderful dream presentation.

I smiled. Lauren made me proud, and I was glad Susie and the children were nowhere to be heard.

You could say that she made lemonade out of a lemon, but that seems way too trite for the years of work on herself that included forgiveness, dedication to help others, and determination to be the person she was created to be and not the "Multiple" that was the result of her early traumatized life.

A QUILT FOR PEACE

Grandmom peeked out the window at all the kids playing in the street. She was watching her grandchildren during their spring break from school. Little Johnny was seven years old, Adam was nine, and Katie eleven. Their downtown Phoenix neighborhood was a rainbow of colors and ethnic families.

"What can we do today?" Johnny asked.

Adam was glued to the television playing video games, and Katie was almost out the door to join the gang outside. Grandmom had to think fast, as the children were already starting to argue.

Adam said he didn't have any friends close to home, that the boys in the neighborhood were bullies and stupid, and no way would he go outside. Katie wanted to go to Rosie's house, as her mom was at work and the girls could do as they pleased. Johnny had slipped out the back door and was already arguing with Keith on the front lawn over who would get to bat first.

Grandmom was getting a headache and thinking that this was going to be a long week. Each child wanted to do something different, no one could agree. Whatever was she to do?

Then there was the pressure to adhere to the rules the kids' parents had told her to enforce. Growing up on a farm had never looked so good to Grandmom. There was always something to do: an animal to feed or play with, a chore to do, or a romp in the hay waiting in the barn.

She had brought a sack of cotton squares, thinking she could work on making a quilt while the children played with their friends. Now she realized that there would be no quiet time unless she could bring order out of this chaos.

Suddenly she had an idea. Maybe she *could* use the cloth squares. Calling her three grandchildren together, she told them she had an idea for a fun project. But, they would need all the children outside for it to work.

"What is it, Grandmom?" they asked suspiciously.

"I can't tell you until all the children outside come up on the lawn and I tell you all together."

"It will never work, I can tell already," said Katie. Adam groaned at the thought of leaving the safety of his house, but Johnny was already out the door rounding up the kids.

As the neighborhood gathered outside, Grandmom brought her bag of squares to them. She held up a few squares and challenged each child to run home and return with a piece of worn out clothing so she could make a square from them.

"Now, it must be a piece of clothing that your mother doesn't mind you having. And," she said, "the more unique and lovely, the more special our quilt will be."

Adam groaned. "That sounds like a girl's project to me."

Katie wasn't sure that making a quilt would be fun and, besides, what would they do with it? Johnny was still running around.

Being somewhat bored, the children caught some of Grandmom's enthusiasm, and first one child went home to look for a scrap of material, and then another.

Grandmom started assembling the squares on a big piece of muslin on the driveway. Soon, the children were eager to see each new arrival and where Grandmom would position their piece.

One girl asked to cut the new offerings to the desired size, another challenged Grandmom as to where the newest pieces looked best. The boys wanted to do the pinning.

Juanita's piece was from an old dance skirt she had had in Mexico. Henry's was from an old grain sack. When Diane brought a piece of old fur, Katie remarked that it was too different to be of use. Grandmom smiled and thought that, indeed, it would add nice texture.

"You see," she said as she began to sew, "all your pieces are made of cloth and are the same inside, just as God made you. The variety makes for a more beautiful finished product. Really, this quilt is a piecing together of all you children in the neighborhood. Wouldn't it be wonderful if the world's grown-ups could work together to create peace like you are doing in making this quilt? With your willingness to try something new, and to work together, you children have helped me have a wonderful day. Now, run along and play."

Their play was more cooperative, and she was thankful that she had chosen to suggest this quilt project instead of suffering because of their chaos. Grandmom smiled as she watched the children agree on a game while she sewed. Often one or the other would come up to view her progress on "their quilt."

After her son and daughter-in-law came home from work, they came outside to watch Grandmom work on the quilt. Neighbors they had never met before stopped by to see this comforter made up of all their own fabrics. Soon Juanita's mom brought over some tacos to share, then there were dolmades from Christina's mom and Adam went in and brought out some chips.

While snacking, the adults talked among themselves as to the best place to display their quilt. First one child's head rose from the games, then another, to see the parents talking amicably. All nodded in happy agreement when the community center was suggested.

Grandmom smiled from inside, where peace resided.

A KNOCK AT THE DOOR

I t was a snowy night in our little Pennsylvania town when I was awakened by a knock at the door. I stirred, not wanting to leave the warm, comforter-covered bed.

My husband, alarmed by the middle-of-the-night disruption, hastily put on his slippers and robe. I followed him downstairs, phone in hand in case I needed to call the police. We peered out the window.

"It's Marcy," I stammered, and opened the door.

She had a wild, frightened deer-like look in her eyes; she had no shoes on and was panting. As she came in she exclaimed, "They're in town, following me, and I didn't know where to go."

In our therapy sessions, Marcy had told me about the cult that had tortured her for most of her childhood. Her parents had been members, as was her grandfather and uncle. At age five, she was made to sit on a wooden hobby horse with a pointed triangle positioned to enter her vagina. Her screams brought no compassion. At age fifteen her father had impregnated her, and when the fetus was almost four months old, the cult aborted it and used it as a sacrifice.

I shuddered when I had heard this story in my counseling office, questioned the veracity as it seemed too horrible to be true, and rejected a colleague's advice to commit her immediately.

But, if it was true, this snowy night when she came to me, I believed the cult was capable of anything. I went into the kitchen and made some hot tea. Marcy soon calmed down, my husband went back to bed, and as she left. I made her promise to call the police if she had any sign of the members.

I couldn't get back to sleep. What was my responsibility here? Marcy had been doing fairly well. She had told her husband that she didn't want to give their new address to her family, explained to her children that their grandparents were not welcome in their new location, and maintained a responsible job as a Registered Nurse.

I kept thinking of her previous therapist who had committed her to a mental hospital. Marcy had been quite cautious in revealing pieces of her story, testing whether I would freak and commit her, as well. The fact that she was married to a successful businessman, though he was always traveling, and maintained a job and home for her two children, kept me listening and being present to her by taking one day at a time in love and faith.

She had shown the ability to dissociate, typical of those who have been abused. I remembered the appointment when she entered the office, an angrier version of herself. She called herself, Peggy, and I was scared when she bragged that she could cut her vagina with the knife she carried in her purse. When she excused herself to go to the bathroom, I called the local mental health crisis team.

Seeing the white coats jolted her back to the Marcy personality. I followed the crisis team's vehicle to the hospital, where I consulted with the local psychiatrist, who I knew quite well. After taking the knife, he and I concurred that Marcy could journey back home where her husband was waiting with dinner guests. Marcy was thankful that I had gone to the hospital and consulted with the doctor, and agreed that we would deal with Peggy in the office.

After the knock-at-the-door evening, Marcy brought her husband to our next session. He had been transferred to another city and they would move soon. He shared his realization that Marcy had had a difficult childhood. He supported the need to cut all ties with her family, and her continued therapy in the new location. Marcy had never risked telling him the gorier details.

She came in alone for two more sessions. She had been through so much, but had come so far with our work together. Still, this would give her an opportunity for a fresh start. She recalled that when she first arrived in our small town, she had gone to a priest for counseling and he had seduced her. Maybe in a new town she could start to trust again and stop looking over her shoulder.

After the move, Marcy phoned to share that the children were thriving in the new city, her husband had yet another promotion, and she was working full-time at the local hospital. She was doing okay without therapy. She missed me, but had internalized faith in herself and the goodness within that she had come to accept.

I was devastated when a phone message revealed that Marcy's daughter had driven onto a bridge in the rain, lost control of her car, and was in critical condition in the hospital. She lived until her dad arrived, and then passed. Marcy had never told him that this girl was the one pregnancy by her father that she had fought to let live. Marcy married soon after, and her husband believed the child was his. He had loved his daughter dearly.

Amazed at how well Marcy dealt with this loss, I admired her courage in continuing a vocation of service and creating a good life. Her marriage was reasonable, made possible by his necessary work travels. Their biological son was doing well in his gifted class, and had adjusted to the loss of his sister.

Marcy told me that she still marveled at my ability to be there for her in those earlier years when she had needed someone strong enough to handle her horrible story; someone to believe in her and to be able to hold her in love. She had even returned to a spiritual community.

Did I believe in her story, or in her? It has been my belief that healing comes when there is an abundance of love, which I equate with God. I hope that the love within and through me, and the trusting relationship we developed enabled her to be the wonderful person she was created to be. Her inspired story will always bless me with gratitude that I was on the other side of the door when she knocked.

A SIGN

I t must be that they liked anchovies on their pizzas! What else could possibly be an omen that these couples were meant for each other? After all, how many of us like anchovies on pizza? And, what more important value, goal, or similarity could be as important when choosing a partner, as both of you liking anchovies?

But, let me tell you more.

Sally curled up on the back seat of the Prescott Shuttle that was taking us to Sky Harbor Airport in Phoenix, Arizona. She clutched her pillow and smiled as I asked where she was headed. I detected nervousness as she whispered that she was off on an adventure — to meet the man she had been e-mailing for the past few months.

I'd heard about those internet romances and that most ended when the risk-takers met face to face. Not wanting to be either a wet blanket or the wise relationship counselor I considered myself to be, I continued our conversation.

She bravely asserted that her return ticket was booked for four days from now, and she doubted they could kill each other in that short of a time. They had planned to meet a couple months down the road, but a long holiday weekend from her work presented an opportunity they couldn't resist.

Finding her story interesting, and ignoring the other Shuttle passenger's rolling eyes, I pressed on. This plumpish red-haired lady in her mid-fifties, I guessed, said she had kept track of a man who had gone to her high school in Mississippi. He was three years older and they had dated, briefly, after her graduation when she had worked as a DJ at the same radio station. The dating ended when his estranged wife sought reconciliation.

Life and marriage brought her across the country to Prescott, Arizona. Then her husband had died after a long, six-year illness. Before he died, he lovingly told her that he hoped she would find someone with whom to share the rest of her life.

Tired from nursing him for those many years, she replied, "Not interested. And besides, how would I find someone at this stage of my life?"

"I'll help," he replied. "And when I find him, I'll send you a sign."

Live goes on, and when one of her friends came to visit, Sally couldn't resist telling her about the e-mails back and forth with this newly-divorced, old acquaintance. Phone conversations had revealed they belonged to the same church, they shared similar goals and values, and they noticed that they finished each other's sentences.

During a shopping trip to the mall, later that day, the first store they went into had a big sign that read, "Joy."

Sally remarked, "Funny ... that was my husband's name."

They had been talking about her Mississippi e-mail friend.

When the next store also had a big "Joy" sign, her friend shouted, "What more of a sign do you need? He told you that he wanted you to be happy!"

So the plans to meet began.

After hearing more of her story, I was beginning to feel more hopeful. And then Sally grinned and shared that they even both liked anchovies on their pizza.

Sally's story triggered a memory of Baltimore, Maryland, and my friend, Pat. Pat loved butterflies, and her home was decorated in orange and black, 1970s colors.

In the 1990s, Pat was dying of cancer and had a similar conversation with her husband about wanting him to find a new partner.

Years passed before he found a wonderful woman, and brought her to Thanksgiving dinner. Into the dining room, flew an amazing orange and black butterfly. Convinced that this was a sign that Pat approved, they made plans for their wedding.

When he called to invite me to the wedding and rave about his bride-to-be, he commented that they even shared a liking for anchovies on their pizza.

I still don't know whether signs from spouses, who have passed, bring people together, or whether compatibility is just finding someone else who likes anchovies on their pizza.

FROM HER MATTRESS TO THE MALL

She sat on the left bottom corner of her mattress for seven years and stared out at the world beyond.

The thought of leaving her room, much less her home, terrified her. Her husband of thirty-eight years brought her morning coffee and a bran muffin before leaving for work each day. Their daughter lived fifty miles away and had invited them for every Christmas since her six-year-old son was born. Though her husband wanted to spend Christmas Day with his grandson and family, he didn't leave his wife. She had tried counseling years before when she was able to leave the house, but it didn't help. And, now, she couldn't even leave her room.

On October 23, 1982, her life changed. She looked up at her husband, standing at the door to their room, and saw his hesitant and fearful expression. His company had told him that he was to receive early retirement, and that Friday would be his last day at work.

Tearfully, but with determination, he announced that, by golly, he was not going to spend the rest of his days as a prisoner in his own home. He had always talked of taking trips in their Lincoln Town car.

Her heart fluttered, her skin was clammy, and no words could come out of her dry mouth. Whatever was she to do? It wasn't that she wanted to stay in this room. She had wanted to go to Canada and hear Jimmy Swaggert. Why, to go shopping in the mall was something she could only dream about. She prayed harder that night than ever before.

She remembered reading an ad in the paper recently about a counselor who worked with panic attacks and agoraphobia. Her heart raced, and her hands were clammy as she reached for her phone. The wind was blowing the trees outside her bedroom window as she listened to the ringing of the phone. "God, please let this counselor be willing to come to my house and help me," she prayed. "Dare I hope that she will be able to do what my family, my church, and friends haven't been able to in the past seven years?"

A calm, pleasant voice answered, and an appointment was arranged to be at her home in two days. She trembled with a combination of hope and fear. What if she could never be helped? What if her husband started traveling without her? How would she cope?

The counselor sat on the right corner of the bed and asked some questions: When had this started? What was the feeling when she first was afraid to leave home? The counselor explained that sometimes people had a terrifying experience in a past life and were vulnerable when an incident in this lifetime occurred.

They talked for awhile and the counselor took out little slips of paper. On each she wrote a step, starting with standing up in the room, and ending with opening the front door. Then the counselor had her visualize doing each of the steps. Each time she felt nervous or anxious, she went back to the previous slip of paper and repeated that step. Her homework was to repeat this exercise at least twice a day until the counselor returned.

She began to have hope. The counselor came once a week. She was eventually able to go out of her room, down the hall, and out the front door. Her body didn't know the difference between visualizing leaving her room, and actually doing it.

She began to believe that her life could be different. Her goal was to spend Christmas Day with her daughter and grandson.

Now that she wasn't sitting on the edge of her bed all day, her husband bought a new mattress. He began to work with her, and soon they were driving a mile, and then five miles, and soon ten miles away from the house toward their daughter's.

She added daily affirmations. She would say, "I thank you, body, for enabling me to safely go out and return to my house." Or, "Thank you, God, I put my trust in you."

She loved being at her daughter's for Christmas. That year, however, she and her husband also went to Canada to hear Jimmy Swaggert and praised the Lord for her healing. When she returned, she went in to the counselor's office for weekly appointments.

She realized that she couldn't just wish for her life to be different, that she had to be involved in the process of change. Just as a mattress benefits from springs to support it, enabling us to have a better night's sleep, we need support in living life. It's good to rid ourselves of mattresses that sag or are old, and no longer serve us.

Visualizing the life we want is powerful. Why, later that week, she phoned the counselor to tell her that she lunched with friends and went shopping at the mall!

BIRDS

I don't know about birds. When I left the Heart Opening ritual at a Brugh Joy conference, I was in an altered state. As part of the ritual, I had meditated, dressed in white, lay on a table while others surrounded me with love and touched me with their healing hands, and heard Brugh say, "Open your heart as never before."

I headed toward the heated swimming pool on this crisp January day, and the trees bowed as I walked. Never before have the rocks moved, the clouds been full of faces, and the birds chirped as though they expected me to talk back.

Birds have always seemed spiritual to me. Butterflies, the symbol of transformation, and we've all read about Jonathan Livingstone Seagull. There are other references to birds, but nothing personal until my close friend, Pat, died.

It was typical of Pat to write out instructions for a celebration in her backyard after her memorial celebration. As per her request, there were lots of balloons around and, of course, butterflies. Most of the one-hundred or so friends were in the house when I went out into the backyard. David, her son-in-law, was chasing the grandchildren around this big backyard that sloped to the lake. Lots of tall trees lined the pathway down to the shore. Pausing to see what had stopped David's activity, I saw his hand point skyward.

There was a bald eagle slowly circling the sky above the yard. Tears streamed down both of our faces. Slowly others came outside and the silent, tearful group could only watch this majestic sight. No one had ever seen an eagle in these parts before. I had a vision of Pat's bald head, the result of her chemo treatments.

After ten whole minutes of circling, the eagle was joined by two more eagles, who escorted our eagle off into the sky beyond. It occurred to us that Pat had been predeceased by her beloved parents. I have read accounts written by people who have "died" and come back to life witnessing to the fact that they were met in their transition by a loved one. So, why couldn't this have been her parents this day?

A year later, my brother lay dying in his Hospice room. As his breathing grew more labored and the nurses said there was no hope, I held his hand and gave him my permission to let go.

Hearing two birds chirping on the window sill, I offered that perhaps our mother and friend, Pat, were waiting for him outside. His breathing slowed until it was no more. I sat by his bedside and prayed that Spirit would receive him. Knowing that he had his doubts about anything beyond this lifetime, I was grateful for what I believed was his freedom from suffering.

He had wanted his remains to be buried above our mother's coffin in the little country churchyard where our grandparents had begun a family plot. Days later at his service, as the cello played in that peaceful setting, a raven insistently seemed to caw its message, "How about that, Sis, there is something beyond after all!"

Later that year, Pat's family was awestruck to observe an orange and black butterfly circle their Thanksgiving dinner table in the middle of their home in Baltimore. Pat loved orange and black. She loved to be with family, especially on holidays. When I was told about this amazing occurrence, all I could do was shake my head and say that I really don't know about butterflies and birds. Do you?

Perhaps, I should say that I really don't know about birds, but I do know that the spirits of those who have transitioned communicate with us whenever we are open to them, and in whatever way they think we will pay attention. So, if I were honest about it, I'd say that I really *do* know about *these* birds.

THE INTERVENTION

She telephoned from Iowa to ask if someone in our agency could do an intervention. The call was referred to me. Her daughter lived in Arizona, was working at one of the casinos, and the mother, a sister, and brother wanted to hold an intervention.

"What was the problem?" I probed.

"Well, she has a young elementary school child, is a single parent, and has a history of gambling." Her gambling had resulted in a loss of twenty-thousand dollars of the family's money, years before, and they weren't up for a repeat. Now I was hearing a reason for an intervention.

Into the conference room they marched: mother, gray hair worn in a bun; sister, avoiding her problem-sister's eyes; and a rather bland brother. As the session progressed, I learned that the former gambler liked working at the casino because it paid well; plus, allowed her to work hours when her child was in school. No, she'd learned her lesson since her previous losing attempt to beat the odds.

The consensus of the family, however, seemed to be that the woman was ruining her life. Specifically how was the question on the table.

Mom moaned that it was a shame that a girl, her daughter, who had a Master's degree in English, was wasting away dealing blackjack in a casino.

"Mom, I am supporting myself and my daughter and, besides, I have written and published a book!"

Looking highly embarrassed, and with a red tinge showing on her neck, the mom whispered that, "how could she tell anyone, much less her bridge group, that her daughter had written a how-to book on achieving multiple orgasms?"

Sis and bro were mostly concerned that she not need any money from them, nor would she need any from mom. What to do?

The usual intervention ending — with the family confronting the sinner with accounts of her waywardness, requiring institutionalization — somehow didn't seem appropriate. The casino worker appeared to be in clear control of her life and even sounded kind of interesting.

I had a flash. Turning to the mom, who had, after all, flown to Arizona from Iowa for our meeting, I proposed that the daughter attend a weekly meeting of my women's growth group for six weeks. That way, I could see that she was stable for a six-week period and then evaluate whether any further meetings, or counseling, would be helpful.

The mom and family were satisfied that some action was being taken, while the daughter was pleased that the action being taken didn't sound too painful. And I was happy that the daughter would be sharing the wisdom from her book with the women's growth group!

Given the ease and speed of this intervention, you might say it was almost orgasmic!

SCREAMING FOR HELP

T he State of Arizona questioned the value of long-term therapy in the current "fix in six sessions" era.

Our staff at Phoenix Interfaith Counseling had invited Gina to come to a staff meeting to attest to how well she was doing on her own after five years of therapy. No longer at state expense in a hospital, there were no bracelets on her wrists to hide her cutting. She was earning money making ceramics and crafts, and she and Rob were almost ready to buy a house in the country. She had a life.

She handed me this poem as she left, and thanked me for enabling her to have a life.

These are her words:

THE VOICES OF GOD
While you are looking at the
Footprints in the sand,

Listen to the voices of God,
Hear the waves of the ocean as
They gently wash against the shore.
Listen to the gentle voice of God,
As he confronts his children.
Hear the thunderous roar of the sea
As it crashes on the rocks.
Listen to the angry voice of God,
As he shouts for the injustices
Done to his children.
Hear the babbling brook
As it meanders upon its way.
Listen to the laughing voices of God,
As he feels the joy of his children.
Hear the spattering of the rain
As it falls from the sky.
Listen to the tormented voice of God,
As he cries for the pain and
Suffering of his children.
Hear the silence of the lake as
Night takes over the noise of day.
Listen to the silent voice of God,
As he mourns for the loss of
His beloved children.
As you leave your footprints
Through life,
Listen to the many voices of God

My mind reflected back five years to the time I met this young woman. Gina had just been released after nine months in the State Mental Hospital. Five feet tall, two-hundred-seventy-six pounds, and old beyond her thirty-three years, her wary eyes held that dull, "I've been drugged for a long time," look.

When she walked into my office for the first time, I immediately noticed the black wrist bands which I imagined hid her slash marks. I was to be her new therapist.

Earlier that morning, I overheard a colleague comment that when she had interned at the State Hospital, Gina was the one patient she never expected to leave. There had been numerous suicide attempts.

Great, I thought.

Gina began to tell her story. She was her father's favorite of four daughters, almost the son he never had. As soon as she came home from school, he started training her on the Arabian horse. She remembers the bright lights that made it possible for them to train into the long nights, and the wet pants when she couldn't hold her pee any longer. Most of all, she remembered the constant drive for the impossible perfection. Her cutting on her wrists helped release the pain of the memories and bring her into the *now*.

And then Eric came into her life. He was an older man who gave her a way out when she was seventeen years old. When I spoke to Gina's mom, she figured Gina's problems started after she and Eric returned from a camping trip.

"Things happened." she said. And the whole thing scared the hell out of her ... not natural.

All Gina would reveal to me was that Eric treated her like his slave, she refused to ever have sex with him again, and she became depressed. Gina ran away, wondering what she had done wrong.

She spent much of her time sitting outside her apartment, smoking cigarettes, and talking to "the children" who lived in her head.

Angel was the child who cried all the time. Charlie Lee helped her. Two of the girls always begged her to "take them home." I came to understand that "home" was reached by dying.

There were two more children, six in all. They were distinct from the "voices," which she also heard. She only experienced one or the other at a time.

The voices often spoke like her parents had. "One day they'll lock you up and throw the key away," was a frequent message that sounded like Dad. Gina alternated between being aggressive or quite passive, like Mom.

Mom had taken the daughters to Sunday school until Gina was seven or eight. Then Mom had a "falling out" with the preacher, who talked about the need to worship the Devil. Gina learned from him

180

about "where the damned go."

Gina's oldest sister was in jail, and Gina said, "That's where the damned go." Another sister was dealing drugs, and the youngest had a small son and lived with their mom. Gina loved her nephew and he would climb up into her lap when his mom was mean.

After her divorce, Gina met a skinny mechanic, who was kind to her, though he was quite self-centered. They married and rented a room near Mom's house. There were arguments when Gina would object to nightly sex and go outside to smoke. She also would talk to "the children."

When Rob came in for a session, he told me that he thought the frequent sex would enable Gina to go to sleep and reduce the need to go outside. Besides, *he* slept better when her body was next to his.

She found out about the blonde he had been having an affair with from her neighbor. They found her before the overdose killed her, and this resulted in her commitment to the Arizona State Mental Hospital. Gina told me that one of the voices told her to take the pills so she could go "home." She thought it had to be better than where she was.

Apparently, Rob was jolted into kindness — he visited Gina regularly in the hospital, and promised faithfulness. But when she was released, he refused to come in for sessions, telling me, "Gina is the messed-up one."

Gina's continued cutting helped her focus her attention away from the pain in her heart. Rob had told her not to cut anymore, but she said, "No one is going to tell me what to do with my body any more." I never did.

She started attending a group in addition to our individual sessions. In group therapy, she told of her belief that Rob stayed with her because they needed her disability check due to his constant loss of jobs. He had a temper and a strong will. Her family disliked him so much they wouldn't even let him in the house at Christmas. His family lived in another state and the one year they went there, Gina cried as she opened her gift, a size eight dress. I doubt this heavyset woman had ever seen a size eight.

Gina became less depressed as our therapy progressed, and she wanted a life. She dreamed of a house in the country, animals to love, woods to walk in, and quiet to calm the cries of the children who lived in her head. She wanted it badly enough to work hard in her sessions.

I had been seeing her for two years when the phone rang one night at 1:30am. I listened to the frightened voice of Gina's neighbor who said that Gina was outside threatening to kill herself. Her friend had never believed her until now and called me for help.

I decided to get up and dressed. My husband insisted on accompanying me to this section of town, full of low-cost motels serving as weekly rentals, drug dealers in the parking lots — and Gina.

She sat on the back end of her pick-up truck with a knife in her hand. I'd brought Ernie, my big brown fuzzy therapy bear. She agreed to trade.

My husband was in the car watching, vowing never to repeat this craziness. Gina couldn't believe I was there. "I love you," I said, "but, I'll never do this again." I never needed to.

Time passed. Gina was able to send "the children" to their mental rooms, convince them that she was okay, and thank them for being there for her when she needed them.

She began to tell her husband how she felt and what she needed. He listened, and started coming in for couple sessions. They learned to function as a team, to set goals and support each other. He started keeping his job. They even made friends with another couple and socialized like regular folks.

One day she brought in a beautiful angel with outstretched arms that she had made in her ceramics class. "This is for all your clients who need to know that there *is* love and help in the world."

My belief is that we all are the voices of God for those who are crying or screaming for help. Are you listening?

WHAT ARE THE CHANCES?

She finally told me about her dad's death. He and her mother went hunting in Pennsylvania when Ann was two years old.

Her parents were having a great time hunting deer with their best friends; a couple they had known for years, when suddenly a shot rang out and her mother heard a crash. She ran to her bleeding husband, turned white, and called for help. Their friends rushed to the scene; he lifted Ann's father over his shoulder as his wife looked at her smoking rifle, stunned.

He died two days later of the gunshot wound close to his heart. My friend, Ann, grew up without a father. Her mother took to drinking and was often found quietly rocking on the front porch swing, smoking one of many cigarettes.

Eventually her mother remarried and Ann had a stepfather. The half-brother who arrived seemed to bond the parents but, my friend, the reminder of an unhappy past, grew up lonely.

Ann and I met in Maryland, miles away from that Pennsylvania town. We were college graduates who worked at the Baltimore City Welfare Department. Eventually we each married, left the Agency, and raised our children together. Ann battled an anxiety disorder for much of her life. We shared the ups and downs of life and remained close, supportive friends. The day came when my husband and I moved from Maryland to a town in Pennsylvania, close to the place where I had grown up, and opened a counseling practice.

One day a young woman came into my office. She cried as she told me that her mother had killed her best friend's husband in a hunting accident years before. Her mother was consumed with guilt and grief.

My client had grown up lonely and self-sufficient. She had kept herself from marrying, or even having a close relationship until now. There was a man in town who had invited her to go on trips out of town with him. My client's initial happiness waned when she learned he was married. She had begun to feel guilty after the man chose not to divorce his wealthy wife and, yet, she still traveled with him.

I wondered if she was afraid to be close to someone available for fear he would leave her or not meet her emotional needs. All of this, as a result of her mother's tragedy.

Months later, after she had summoned up the courage to sever the relationship with her married man, my client wrote a feature article for the newspaper about her healing journey through counseling, and the woman she had seen.

She never knew "the rest of the story" about the other little girl, now living in Maryland who was my friend, left without a father that fateful day, affecting both daughters.

What are the chances that I would be involved in both lives as I lived in two different states? How many times have you asked a similar question in your life about an unbelievable coincidence? The book, *The Celestine Prophecy*, begins with the words, "There are no coincidences." What is there then?

I believe we have opportunities in life to be instruments of healing if we are open to them. Perhaps we even come into this lifetime with a job to do. Was mine chance or Divine Order?

AN EXPERIENCE OF ONENESS

I planned a trip to Milan to view Da Vinci's, *The Last Supper*.
Forty-five years had passed, and a restoration performed on the
piece, since I had seen it.

Reservations were necessary, so I made them for my husband and
myself many months ahead. We scheduled this trip because our son
was an art professor at Penn State University and was to be in Todi,
Italy, with a group of students for a seven-week summer session.

I fingered and read, over and over, the confirmation for 6:15pm, on
July 3rd. I could hardly wait for our trip.

The instructions said to be at the ticket office at the Basilica de Santa
Maria no later than 6:00pm. I made sure that our arrival at the hotel
in Milan was early afternoon, so there would be plenty of time to take
in some sights and not be late at the Basilica.

When we arrived in Italy, our son was excited to take us to his
favorite spiritual site, the Basilica of St. Francis in Assisi. My husband

and I loved art and had studied St. Francis's moving poem that begins, "Lord, let me be an instrument of Thy peace." We expected to be moved by this visit.

We were, indeed, awed by the architecture of the building, the lovely music inside, and we felt the intense energy of the worshipers that Sunday morning. This was what I expected to experience in Milan and, yet...

We arrived at the ticket office at the Basilica de Santa Maria even earlier than required. There were 24 people checking in, and we all were led past the crowd of disappointed folks looking wistfully at the "SOLD OUT" signs.

At precisely 6:15pm, the first set of three sliding glass doors, with security bars on them, opened and we were admitted to a room no larger than an elevator. As those doors closed, electronically, another set opened. We could no longer see anyone ahead of us or behind.

As the third set of sliding doors opened, we walked into a huge room with white-washed walls. There it was – *The Last Supper* — covering one entire end wall.

I slowly moved toward the rail separating us from the painted wall. All twenty-four of us easily fit along this metal rod separating us from Jesus and the twelve disciples.

Having read *The Da Vinci Code*, my eyes focused upon the person seated to the right side of Jesus. Was it a disciple, or Mary Magdalene? The hum of the room's humidifier was the only sound penetrating my reflection.

The others moved silently to the other end of the room, where *The Crucifixion* painting consumed the wall. I stayed at the rail before *The Last Supper*. I noticed that the guards were focused mostly on the Japanese tourists and their cameras at the opposite wall. I noted the "No Photography" sign, clicked the no flash setting on my camera, and angled the digital upwards from my waist and clicked, hoping that it caught something to help me remember this moment forever.

With nothing more to think about, or to do, my eyes fastened upon the painting. I began to feel pulled into it. There appeared an aura around the head of Jesus. His eyes pierced mine. My heart was pounding louder than the humidifier. I was THERE. Time stood still, and there was no then or now, just a *oneness* I had never experienced before.

The bell, announcing the end of our visit, jarred my experience and brought me back to the present. Or, had I been in the present, past, and future all at the same moment? If so, was there a place in consciousness where it was still happening and my level of consciousness, at that one intense moment, allowed me to experience timelessness? We all have had experiences we call, *déjà vu*. Could it be that during those times, time is standing still and we are "in the experience," once again?

My husband gently held my arm and moved me toward the door. The glass doors opened and we moved into the first of three more rooms leading to the, inevitable, gift shop. Our, much anticipated, fifteen minutes were up. It had seemed much longer.

That night, I was roused from sleep at 6:15am. Not yet awake, I was again in the Oneness. I had come to see the painting; instead, I had felt present with Jesus, and the others, in a warm sea of peace, love, and belonging. There was no separation of time or space.

Our human world is multi-dimensional. However, could there be Oneness in Spirit, where we are not only a part of all that is, but in that realm, could everything be present?

I thought I had been pulled to Milan to see the restoration of this great painting. Instead, I had been gifted with a very special experience of Oneness.

A COMMON THREAD

Responding to a recent personal challenge gave me an opportunity to reflect on my increased faith in intuition, and my belief that we each have the inner resources to meet the challenges that life presents.

As often happens in our lives when we are paying attention, our minds wander back to incidents in our pasts that have a common thread; incidents that seem to affirm our beliefs and help us along our spiritual journey.

Not too long ago, I watched a children's movie, *Kung Fu Panda.* Watching it with my grandchildren, I was mesmerized by the story as it unfolded. The connection between my own experiences, and those of that animated Panda, were uncanny as he pushed himself beyond his apparent limitations to finally see the wisdom that came from within.

Of course, the literal dream of Panda becoming the Dragon Master was not my dream; however, his triumph over a menacing challenge, his eventual belief in himself, and his understanding that there is no "magic" answer, had a very familiar ring.

I smiled to myself as I settled into my chair to spend more time with this lovely memory when a second incident gently nudged the Panda to a quiet corner of my mind.

This memory took me back to a cruise on the Baltic Sea to Russia. The long airplane ride had left me without a book to read on the ship, so I scampered to the ship's library and Caroline Myss's book, *Sacred Contracts*, caught my attention. I looked forward to a quiet read on the deck.

A lecture later that day showcased the delicate *papier-mâché* boxes painted by Russian village artists with brushes made of rabbit hairs. Allowing myself one special vacation purchase, I eagerly went to the evening display of these treasures, and was immediately drawn to a small black hexagonal box with red and gold figures painted on all sides.

None of the other treasures spoke to me the way this one did, and I stood in line, eagerly waiting to ask the lecturer/salesman about the fairy tale depicted on the box.

"Why, it's the one of Vasalisa and Baba Yaga."

I was not familiar with this story, but he assured me it was one of the most common in his country. Unfortunately, the crush of buyers prevented his telling me the story.

Relaxing on a lounge chair with my book the next day, I could not stop thinking of my new treasure packed in my suitcase, and my eagerness to find the fairy tale once I returned home to Google.

Imagine my surprise, when on Page 45 of *Sacred Contracts*, the tale of Vasalisa and Baba Yaga appeared. Caroline Myss used this story as a reminder for us to listen to our inner voice, or intuition, as a guide in our lives.

The story of Vasilisa begins when she is a young girl caring for her dying mother. Before the mother passes, she gives her daughter a tiny magical doll. "Should you lose your way, or be in need of help," her mother said, "ask this doll what to do. You will be helped."

After the mother's death, the story parallels that of our *Cinderella* when her father remarries. Vasalisa finds herself living with a mean stepmother and two resentful stepsisters. The story tells how Vasalisa is sent off through the menacing forest to get fire to warm the hearth from the wicked witch, Baba Yaga.

When the stepmother extinguished the fire in the home, it symbolized her snuffing out the warmth in the family.

Vasalisa returns home, with the doll's help, from her frightening encounter with Baba Yaga, and, just like Kung Fu Panda, finds a new awareness of her inner power.

As I reflect on these two incidents, I can see how we all find our own wisdom within. The Panda's came from the Kung Fu Master. Vasalisa's wisdom came from her mother's doll. Mine derives from the One Presence.

Why did I choose that particular book? Why that box as my souvenir? Did I respond to guidance and my free will to make choices?

I believe that I am growing in my ability to listen to those thoughts within. I am convinced those inner nudges come from guidance. And since I surrender more and more my need to try to "make" things happen, the resources to meet life's challenges flow more freely.

We all have a sacred contract to fulfill in this lifetime. It seems that when we get out of our egos, are more allowing and open to intuition, and act out of love, we raise our consciousness into the Oneness. Imagine, all this wisdom from a Chinese Panda and a Russian fairy tale, as told by an American story teller! How about that common thread?